A Mountain to Climb

Growing up in the twenties, thirties and beyond

The true accounts of the early lives of one couple
and their individual experiences during World War II

by Nora and John Mountain

D1460427

Credits

First published 2009. This updated edition published 2010

ISBN: 978-1-4452-1452-8

Acknowledgements

Our thanks to our family for their help in producing this book - Liz, Don, Judith, Martin and Jon

Cover illustration is based on the January 1944 (Vol.3) edition of the 'Marking Time' newsletter originally accredited to D Gold. Re-drawn for this book by Helen Aldous.

Any profits from the publication of this book will be donated to Wakefield Hospice (www.wakefieldhospice.org)

For updates and further information please visit our website:
www.amountaintoclimb.co.uk

In memory of
Sergeant John Leonard Hartley (RAF)

Shot down over Belgium
September 1944

Introduction

As the period of our lives seems to be passing into history we were persuaded by family members and friends to attempt to write a true account of our experiences during the so-called hungry 20's and 30's and the trauma of living through the Second World War.

Happily we are profoundly thankful to have been able to do this over a period of several months when our memories have served us well.

It is really only a mirror of what millions of others, both here in the UK and in the Commonwealth endured until the end of hostilities. We feel incredibly lucky to have survived for so long in reasonably good health - now into the 22nd year of living in our comfortable sheltered bungalow.

Nora and John Mountain
January 2010

Fig 1: John's mother, Dorothy with baby Millie (John's sister)

John's Story

Chapter 1

Until quite recently, I always had some doubt about the exact location of my birth, which was on 11th April 1920. Dad had told me it was in one of an old row of cottages in Alverthorpe village, which was near and at right angles to Colbeck's Mill Dam. This was off Green Lane, which in turn led to the main Batley Road. The cottages, like many others in villages in the Wakefield area, would have been built in the 19th or even 18th centuries.

My late sister, Millie, always insisted my birthplace was in another old cottage in Blacksmith's Fold. This was a roughly surfaced, unmade street which ran uphill from the main Batley Road for about 200 yards and containing about two-dozen old cottages, built on either side of the street. I have now ascertained, by obtaining a copy of my birth certificate, that I was born at 189 Batley Road, Wakefield. This came as a big surprise to me! The house, part of a small terrace, is no longer there - today it is a grassed area.

My first memory, around three or four-years-old, is of running about in the street. I fell and badly cut my knee on a stone - I still have the scar today.

Dad was born John William Mountain. His parents were Mary and William Mountain, his father was a stone mason. Dad had a brother, Ernest, and two sisters, Sarah and Annie. According to Dad his father used to take off on the road for months at a time undertaking casual stone masonry work during his wanderings - leaving the family almost destitute. He was eventually found dead by the roadside. I have no information as to the circumstances or whereabouts of his death.

At this point I must thank my nephew and niece for doing family research on both mine and my wife's families. Previously having only very faint knowledge some of this information came as a revelation to both of us, having lived so many years - now being in our late eighties.

My mother's maiden name was Dorothy (Dolly) Evelyn Yorke. Born in Sheffield she moved to Walsall (Staffordshire) before the First World War. Her father was a traveller, now known as a 'rep' and she had two sisters; Millie and May. Just prior to the First World War starting in 1914 my mother's family again moved, this time to Castleford where she must have met Dad. They were married there in January 1916 during his leave from the army. He was serving in the Royal Engineers.

Dad was born in 1888, at Snow Hill (Wrenthorpe) and worked as a builder's labourer after leaving school up until he went off to war. At that time and for many years into the twentieth century labouring was extremely hard work. Millie was born in late 1916 - and christened Mildred Edith. At the time the family was still living at 20 Blacksmith's Fold.

Dad survived the war but conditions throughout the 1920's were grim. There were massive food shortages and widespread influenza epidemics all over Europe in which millions died. I believe he kept working in the building trade but in those days and indeed well into the 20th century there was no recompense for time lost due to bad weather. To make matters worse, like so many people in hard times, he spent some of his wages on drink. This was at the expense of his family - which must have been a miserable time for my mother. After I came along in 1920 it must have been doubly so.

Later in my life Auntie Millie told me I was given very little chance of survival after birth - being born so puny and weak-chested. She said I was only kept alive at first by having daily vinegar baths. Whether this was true I have no idea. Like so many old remedies, it may actually have saved my life. All I know is I was a sickly, weak child up to leaving school in 1934.

I have no recollection of my brother, Eric, being born in 1923 but I know he was born with a deformity - having one foot badly twisted outwards. At one-year-old he had corrective surgery at Clayton Hospital. This must have been quite unusual then and was only partly successful - it left him with a lifelong limp. In spite of this he worked as a plumber before being called into the army. He was medically graded Class-B so he didn't have to serve overseas but was able to follow his trade at HQ Eastern Command. One of his jobs was working on Churchill's underground war room. Now 85 years old, he is living in Sussex after a good career with Mid-Sussex Water.

From the age of four I have happy memories of attending my first infants school, a very small old stone building adjoining Colbeck's Mill in Flanshaw Lane. I also recall visiting my mother's friend, Lizzie Farrar, who had a sweet shop at the corner of the Fold and Batley Road. Still aged four, I have a very clear memory of kneeling at mother's bedside in January 1925 but not realizing she was gravely ill. She passed away early in March of abdominal influenza and gastro enteritis, aged 29 years old. She left a husband and three young children, one little more than a baby - an absolute disaster for us. I remember mother's funeral, walking up Church Hill behind her coffin with no cabs to ride in then.

Millie, by then nine-years-old bore the brunt of it. She was expected to look after me, take me to school and take Eric to Lizzie Farrar's. She then had to see to us until Dad came home from work. I have no idea how we managed for meals.

Soon after my mother's death I got scarlet fever and was taken to Park Lodge Lane Hospital, which was also a workhouse for destitute people. Every morning I was given a cup of liquid liquorice powder (a widely used laxative). One day I spilled this on the bedsheet and was given a good smacking by the nurse and marched off screaming to the laundry room where I went through the motions of washing the sheet.

On returning home (probably near Christmas) I was given a popular boy's sweet treat - a 'smoker's outfit' which was made entirely from liquorice. In those days there was no mention of smoking damaging your health - more the opposite!

Soon afterwards, Dad moved us to an even smaller and even older cottage, just across the street. I suppose that would have been because it was less rent. It was really only a hovel, as indeed many of the other houses were. He had managed to get work near home on the new housing estate being built further up Batley

Road. I remember seeing him at work, carrying bricks and mortar up ladders all day long and having only one break - for lunch. Eventually, the situation must have overpowered him because my next memory is of being homeless. I don't know if he had got behind with the rent payments and we were turned out or if we left voluntarily. We then moved into lodgings in Wrenthorpe.

Millie was taken in by the Hudson family who were related by marriage to Dad's sister, Annie. The Hudsons owned one of the two village fish shops and Millie was to spend the next several years as an unpaid servant, helping in the shop after school.

Aged 10 and while attending Wrenthorpe Council School, as it was then called, Millie was allowed to sit for the County Minor Scholarship. This was held every spring at Outwood Ledger Lane School. She passed the exam, allowing her entry into secondary education. Locally this could be at either Wakefield Girls High School or at Thornes House School and would mean staying in education to 16 years old. At that time the elementary education leaving age was 14. Her guardians (or, should I say employers) would not allow her to go. Having reached the top class she spent another three years more or less learning what she already knew. On leaving she started work in the noisy weaving shed at Colbeck's Mill. At 16 she managed to break away from her fish-shop life and went to live with Auntie Annie and family and then to Auntie Millie's in Flanshaw until her marriage and a permanent home during the Second World War.

Fig 2: John's sister, Millie, aged 18

Returning to my memory of being homeless - I next remember living with Mrs. Gott, an elderly widow and her unmarried son, Ernest. Dad had known Ernest in his earlier days, having been brought up in Wrenthorpe. The house was in another very old terrace at the top of Bunkers Hill, built in Victorian times with no hot water facility or indoor toilet. There was a brick-built block of 'earth closets' with wooden seats and a large galvanized metal bucket below, emptied regularly by the Council - what a job! Infested in warm weather by flies and other insects, each one shared by two or even three families - a sanitary inspector's nightmare! Rubbish disposal was done through another brick building with one open side through which the rubbish and ashes from the coal fires were thrown. Dad had left his house building job and Ernest Gott took him to work with him on night shift down one of the area's pits (I don't know which). This was 1926 - the year of the General Strike. This brought yet more widespread poverty among the working classes, which continued well into the thirties.

When I was six years old (Eric would be only three) we were soon on the 'homeless road' again. Whether the pit work hadn't suited Dad or he hadn't been giving Mrs. Gott enough money for our keep I have no idea. I don't remember us going to Wrenthorpe School at this time, but we may have attended the infant classes briefly and when Millie would have been able to take us - she was living nearby. Before we left the village I remember dragging a small, two wheeled cart and going with Mrs. Gott to a prominent landmark called Lindale Hill to search for bits of coal left lying near the surface, after it had been outcropped in earlier years.

Dad probably had some of his father's wanderlust. We must have first walked to the Leeds Road and taken a one penny tram ride to the terminus at Thwaite Gate, just short of Hunslet. This was the regular service which ran from The Castle pub in Sandal. It was replaced by buses in 1933 - which extended the route into Leeds. We set off walking again - Dad carried Eric - for the two miles to Holbeck. We stopped at another hovel terraced house occupied by an Irishman who Dad had known and visited in his building trade days. This was the time when many Irishmen had immigrated to the Leeds area to find employment doing mostly digging jobs on building sites.

We were only allowed to stay one night during which I vaguely remember sleeping on the floor, then it was back on the road, with Dad still carrying Eric, and me staggering along behind. Why we finally reached Pudsey, two or three miles away, and for what purpose, I never knew. I do remember walking up the steep hill from what is now part of the Leeds Ring Road and calling at a butcher's shop, where the butcher must have taken pity on us as he gave us polony and bread. My memory is a complete blank as to how we managed to get back to Wakefield.

My memory picks up later at a better type of terrace house with, wonder of wonders, a bathroom. This was the first we had ever seen and we were welcomed by a very nice lady in white nurse's uniform. She was the matron of this small, council-run children's home and we were told to address her as Mrs. Gilverthorpe. This house is still in existence today and is situated off Westgate, at the bottom of Back Garden Street. Dad must have finally admitted defeat and put us into care, which might have been a better course of action for us after Mother died. Eric and I have always been in full agreement on this, as were some of our other relations.

In blissful ignorance and being given baths and decent second-hand clothing we were two very happy kids. This was a Saturday and before Dad left he promised to visit us every weekend. We soon felt at home with the other children - I can't remember how many there were but I recall no more than about eight.

On the Monday I was taken with the others to Piccadilly School. This was an old stone building, just below the railway bridge and long since demolished to make way for the new road leading to Ings Road. Eric was still only three and was well looked after - not yet old enough for school. I have happy memories of running under the bridge to school with the others. I also remember visiting Bede House, another small home on College Grove Road, where we were allowed to play with the children. The building still exists today - now converted into flats.

In 1927, possibly in mid-summer, (I remember having turned seven in April), Dad came and told us we were leaving the home. He had got a house and a new job - otherwise he wouldn't have been allowed to take us away. A bus ride took us to 35 School Lane, Wrenthorpe, one of a pair of cottages and our home for the next 10 years. I have a book about the village in olden times and it seems almost certain it was one of several 18th century pottery workers' cottages in School Lane. Like the ones in Alverthorpe, it could only be described as a hovel. There to greet us was someone who Dad said was to be our new mother (in reality our step-mother) - they had recently married. She was of Irish descent but was born in Providence Street, Wakefield and was about 38-years-old.

By today's standards, it wouldn't have been fit for use as a dog kennel - although Eric and I must have been too young to realise this. With just one room it had a small storage place for coal, a stone staircase leading from the one outer door to the one bedroom, an ancient oven range combined in the fireplace, a stone sink in one corner with a cold tap, a small ancient gas-ring and a gas light fitting. The furniture must have been given to Dad - it certainly wasn't worth buying. There was an old wooden armchair, a rocking chair, two small wooden chairs for Eric and me, a monstrosity of a sideboard, a very ancient mangle, and a table. There was just room for the coal delivery man to squeeze through between the table and stair wall to dump the weekly bag in the rear coal place, with the dust flying over everything. The cottage was owned by Ted Cave, a village joiner and undertaker. The rent was two shillings and eleven pence per week (15 pence today). Infested with beetles - 'black clocks' in the Yorkshire dialect - just like many more in the village at that time it was totally unfit. It wasn't until the late thirties when a massive slum clearance started that we were able to move into a brand new council house.

Dad had gone back to work for Furness and Render - local builders, who were still doing Beverley's (Wakefield) Brewery work. This was maintenance, modernising, and building of three new pubs, this suited him fine. When he had money beer was readily available at 6d a pint (2½p) and the New Wheel Inn was only 100-yards from the cottage. I remember Eric and I being quite happy at first - having new playmates and the freedom to roam about the village. Things soon started to go downhill with the 'demon drink' taking over. It was the building trade custom for small firms to pay wages at 12-noon on Saturdays at the normal end of the working week. Instead of Dad coming straight home, he made a bee-line for the New Wheel, often coming home drunk at 3pm (closing time). This usually caused a row with our step-mother who was still working at Holdsworth's Spinning Mill and obviously didn't like it. He would then sleep it off and pacify her by taking her to the evening pub session. This would often lead to ending the day with another row - causing us to cry. Everything would then be calm all week as the money had run out but we came to really dread the week-end eruptions.

The food situation was far from good. Breakfast was invariably two slices of bread and dripping and a mug of tea, sweetened from a single tin of condensed milk, which was expected to last the whole week. Dripping is the fat that was run off the Sunday joint and allowed to solidify. We never saw fresh milk. The main meal was often fish and chips - two or three times a week. Sunday was usually best, when they were both at home.

On our first Monday at 'home', we attended the village school to which Eric (then aged four) went. This had an infants for three to six year olds and a main school, which was divided into what were known then as Standards, taking seven to fourteen year olds. Still only seven, I was put in Standard 1. Although the school was quite old even then it stood another 80 years or more, before only recently being demolished. The teaching staff was both male and female and they were very strict but fair. The cane was liberally used for any misdemeanour and for making mistakes - as I soon found out for spelling one word wrongly. The classes were also for both sexes with about even numbers I can remember being horrified the first time I had to sit next to a girl but I soon got used to it!

From this time and for the next five years, we were left alone from 7.00am. We would go to Auntie Annie's or Grandma's until school time - both lived nearby. On dark winter evenings we went to a kind lady next door. Exams were held every six months at school and, depending on the results, you either went up or down a class. I must have shown promise because I jumped a class to Standard 3 and by 1930 was in the top class - Standard 8, like Millie. Eric also achieved this in 1933.

On Sundays we went to St. Anne's Sunday School classes, which were held in a small former school. After this we were marched up the road to the morning church service but allowed to then leave halfway through in case we got bored with the sermon. Then it was back to afternoon Sunday School lessons. Every year there were book prizes for good attendance and I still possess three of these.

At 10-years-old, I decided to try and join the church choir. Dad took me to see Harry Wilde, the choirmaster and owner of one of the two ropeworks in the village. He gave me a trial at the Wednesday evening practice. I was accepted and soon learned to read music, having already learned a bit at school. I sang alongside two boys who were to become lifelong friends - Leonard Hartley and Jack Carlisle - we would also get together during school holidays.

In February 1931 I was allowed to sit the County Minor Scholarship at Outwood and passed - just like Millie had done. I had the option of going to Wakefield Grammar School (Queen Elizabeth Grammar School - as it's now called) or to Thornes House in Wakefield Park. Dad tried to persuade me to get an early morning paper round - no doubt with family finances in mind! However, I stuck to my guns and not without a few tears from me, he finally relented and I was accepted at QEGS, ready to start in September.

Of course, the problem of lack of money soon became apparent - I had no new clothes, only the obligatory school cap. Things became better after about a year when Dad, being a member of the local British Legion branch, was able to get me a clothing grant. After being measured by the local chairman, I was given a full outfit which sufficed until I left. Officially, under the terms of the scholarship, all books and other items were supplied free but there was always something, like sports clothing and the odd book which wasn't covered. Trying to get Dad to supply the money made life difficult.

It would have been possible to obtain a bus fare grant if you lived at least two miles from the school, but I was closer, so I walked with another boy from the village. There was a one-and-a-half hour lunch-break and I also walked home for that; a total of about seven miles a day. My first class was Form 3-Upper, and some of the pupils were the fee-paying sons of local businessmen, two being sons of the junior school headmaster, Reverend Baines. The school head was AJ Spilsbury, brother of the famous pathologist, Sir Bernard. I did quite well academically - coming out near the top in English and French. When I moved up to 4-Upper in 1932 things became more difficult. This was mainly through my being absent with minor illnesses, like persistent earache and chest colds. It was also due to taking more school subjects, like trigonometry and ancient Greek.

Eric had now moved into the senior school at Wrenthorpe and would soon be taking the scholarship exam. At 12-years-old, I was having a busy life, doing at least an hour's homework, and two nights attending choir practice and confirmation classes. I was duly confirmed at Ardsley Parish Church by the Bishop of Wakefield, which led to attending 8.00am holy communion, Sunday School and both morning and evening services.

That same year I was given a school meal grant and was able to dine with the boarders at School House. This was very good and was overseen by Mr and Mrs Spilsbury. I really missed the meals during school holidays as the home food situation hadn't improved. In August our step-mother went away for a few days and arrived back from the maternity home with our half-sister, Annie. Now there were five of us living in what could only be described as squalor - all five of us sleeping in the same room. This situation was to last another five years until, in 1937, the cottage was finally condemned as unfit for habitation - along with most of the others in School Lane. We were then given a new three-bedroomed house on the new estate.

Given the non-existent hygiene it was a minor miracle how we survived those five years without going down with all sorts of disease. Dad got pneumonia and his lungs were permanently damaged but he still managed to keep drinking and smoking before finally succumbing to lung cancer in 1955.

On a lighter note, Eric passed the scholarship but decided not to take advantage of it. He left school at 14 and got work immediately as an apprentice plumber. In the main hall of the school there was a large wall board, with all scholarship winners dating back to the 1890s printed in gold lettering. I think we were the only family to have all three of us named. It will no doubt have been destroyed with the demolition.

From an early age Eric became a member of a well-known brass band. He played cornet - something he continued in later life at his home town in Burgess Hill, Sussex.

In 1933, although my reports were not so good, I again advanced to form-5A, where I was to become even more stressed with extra lessons. These had to be learned in preparation to sitting the school certificate exam. This was taken before leaving at 16 or carrying on to study for university. Early in 1934, I had got to such a state where I was actually dreading attending anymore and Dad decided to try to get permission for me to leave at 14. This was no easy matter as, without very good reason, the Education Authority demanded a fee of nine guineas - an impossibility for us. However, we managed to get an appointment to see Doctor Potts, the Chief Medical Officer at County Hall and, after hearing how unhappy I was and of my poor health, he waived the fee and allowed me to leave.

No longer having the worry of having to carry on for two more compulsory years at school, I soon started to feel better. Dad, possibly having the family finances in mind, suggested I try to get a job. At the time unemployment was very high during the early thirties depression years. Owing to my poor physical condition Dad thought I might try for an office job. First we went to Sharphouse's, provision merchants in town, who offered me 8 shillings a week as a junior clerk. We rejected that as most firms were paying 10 shillings as a starting rate. Then we went off to Sydney Raines, structural engineers - the only job offered was blacksmith's apprentice, at 8 shillings and 6 pence a week, so also a non-starter. There was another opportunity - Dad had got work with another small builder, newly moved into the village, building 12 semi-detached houses. Two joiners, also from Leeds, offered to take me on as an apprentice at 10 shillings a week (50p today) so that became my first job.

I learned to use a saw and hammer doing small jobs, like creosoting joists, plugging into brickwork joints, hammering in wood plugs for later fixing of skirting boards and picture rails. By collecting for two months from my two shillings-a-week pocket money I was able to put a deposit on a bike at Curry's tiny shop in the Bull Ring. It was a racing type with drop handlebars and narrow wheels - very popular at the time. My employers were two brothers from Old Farnley, Leeds and one needed to go there to another site and took me with him. This was with the provision I made my own way there. Being still late summer I decided to bike it, leaving home at 7.00am to cover the eight miles. The fresh air job must have got me fit because I had no problems doing this. I also benefitted from being given an excellent dinner every day at my boss' house nearby. A few weeks into the job I was on my way home in pouring rain when my front wheel got stuck in tramlines. This was as I turned a corner into Morley town centre - throwing me over the top of the handlebars. Luckily I wasn't hurt but got home exhausted and tearful. Dad wouldn't let me go again - so that became the end of my short career as a joiner!

By this time Dad had moved back to work for one of the partners who had done Beverley Brewery's work. They had split into two firms and the one my dad worked for had started with his son - building ten houses. They offered to take me on as an apprentice bricklayer, but not bound. This was the term used to keep an apprentice until fully qualified at 21-years-old. This meant that I could leave or be sacked any time at two hours' notice - which eventually worked in my favour. However, if I thought I would immediately start to lay bricks, I was quite disillusioned. I was given a shovel to help in mixing concrete and mortar by hand on a large wooden staging. There were no concrete mixers in those days except for in the very large building firms. I often wonder how I coped in my weakling condition but after two or three months I was given tools and put to work between two bricklayers. They gave me a hard time, as was usual then but I soon learned the basics and started to enjoy it.

After about a year I was sent out on my own to do small maintenance jobs, like pointing brickwork. One job was pointing the whole front of the local butcher's house and shop and nearby grocer's shop. I did this using ladders reared up on the pavement with people passing to and fro - a situation which would not be tolerated now. I was becoming fairly good at actual bricklaying, working on several really good private houses. By 17 I was able to go elsewhere as an 'improver' - the term then used for the partly-qualified. The trade was still quite depressed until the late thirties, there being not a lot of local authority work being done. Several small local firms were kept busy building private houses. I had no difficulty finding another job, being better paid by the hour, earning about £1.50 a week, then a good wage for a 17-year-old.

Our home life started to improve in 1937 when we were given a new three-bedroom council house on the Wrenthorpe estate at 10 shillings per week rent. Dad grumbled that it was too much but, as I was contributing more to the housekeeping and Eric had left school and got a job as a plumber's apprentice, it wasn't a hardship. That is with the sad exception that Dad's appetite for beer and cigarettes had not diminished. He often borrowed from me during the week without giving it back, causing friction between us.

Between 1936 and '39, I changed firms five more times - getting a little more money each time. I ended up at Pinderfields Emergency Hospital site, earning 1 shilling and 6½ pence per hour - at the time the tradesman's rate was only a penny more.

Chapter 2

I had kept in touch with Jack and Len from choirboy days. We went to the cinema together on Saturdays even though they were both still at Grammar School until 1937. It was then that Jack became an apprentice electrician and Len went to Stanley Council, studying to become a sanitary inspector. In 1938, with war looming on the horizon, there was plenty of building work - both on underground shelters and air-raid wardens' posts, built on the surface. I worked on several of these before the Pinderfields site for my final six months as a civilian.

On September 3rd 1939, it was a beautiful sunny Sunday morning and I went for an early walk. I arrived back home to hear a statement on the wireless by Prime Minister, Neville Chamberlain, at 11.00am. Our Government had already given a guarantee to come to Poland's aid, if attacked by Germany and this had happened two days earlier. Mr Chamberlain said, 'I have to tell you all that this country is now at war with Germany.' This announcement marked the start of a six-year struggle for millions of people.

That same evening my friend Len and I went into town to meet our friend, Jack, who two months before at 18 years old, had

Fig 3: John, aged 18.

volunteered for the Territorial Army. He was with the 1st/4th King's Own Yorkshire Light Infantry - they were stationed in the George Street drill hall, before being sent out to France. After Jack's posting it became just Len and I who met at the weekends, usually going to the cinema Saturday evenings, and strolling in the town or park Sunday evenings, as did most teenagers.

A total blackout had been imposed on the whole country, making it more difficult getting around after dark. This arrangement lasted until early November, when on Saturday the 11th, after seeing the film 'Gunga Din' at the Empire Cinema, we started chatting to two girls, telling them our names. They were Nora Watson and Dorothy Margison. We stayed together until it was time to walk home and arranged to meet them again on the following Saturday, when I walked Nora home and Len took Dorothy. I asked Nora if we could meet every weekend but she said 'no' at first - it would have to be just Tuesday evenings as she wished to be with Dorothy at weekends. This went on for a few more weeks, during which time Len had volunteered for the RAF and was accepted. Nora and I became closer and were meeting Tuesdays and weekends. So, with both my friends gone and me knowing I would be called up anyway when I reached 20 - I also decided to volunteer.

I went to the RAF recruiting office on Vicar Lane in Leeds. I passed the preliminary medical but was then rejected because I had not attained School Certificate standard which I would have sat at 15. Early in the New Year, I went to Leeds again to the Royal Engineers recruiting office, as I had been told having a trade would be accepted. All I got upon telling them my age was, 'come back when you are 20'.

I didn't try anything else as I knew I would be called up anyway within a few months. I was then enjoying working on the Pinderfields site for the contractors, William Birch of York. I was also enjoying going steady with Nora and spending time at weekends in her home. All too soon 11th April came - my 20th birthday and in early May I received a letter instructing me to report to Huddersfield for a Medical where I was graded 'A-1'.

Then came the disaster in France and the Dunkirk evacuation. Although over 300,000 troops were safely brought back, a large number of infantrymen were killed or captured, making it almost inevitable that I would be called into an infantry unit. Sure enough, early in June 1940, I was ordered to report to the Green Howards depot in Richmond, North Yorkshire. On 12th June I finished work after being paid up by the foreman, Harry Smith. He later joined the RAF and sadly lost his life.

Meanwhile, Nora and I agreed to become engaged and that same evening went to Harland's jewellers to buy her a ring. We then parted the following evening - facing a very uncertain future.

Fig 4: John - the army recruit (1940).

Fig 5: Green Howards Recruit Platoon at Richmond - June 1940
John is indicated by the arrow on the photography

I'm not sure how I reached Richmond the following morning, but I think it was by train to Catterick and about a hundred of us were then taken by army lorry to Richmond Barracks. The first person to speak to me inside the gates, was Captain Hedley Verity, the famous Yorkshire and England slow bowler, who greeted each of us in turn, a true Yorkshire gentleman. He sadly lost his life while leading an attack on a German-held field farmhouse on Sicily in July 1943. He died of his wounds after being taken prisoner. Most of the new intake, as we were called, had been called up with the 26-year age group - only a few of us were 20. The remainder of that day was spent in drawing kit and short Lee Enfield rifles - which had been stored in the armoury after the First World War.

Fig 6: Green Howards Depot Company - Richmond 1940

The only uniform available was the ill-fitting fatigue dress and we were confined to barracks for the first two weeks until the battle dress arrived. This was lucky as we wouldn't have been in good enough condition to go anywhere else after the hectic training schedule. The NCO instructors were all 1st World War veterans, who really put us through the mill in order to get us fully fit. Reveille was at 6.15am, then it was drill, physical training and weapon and bayonet training until 6.00pm. After that we had to turn out for an hour at dusk. This was the invasion scare time across the whole country - when it was thought there would be massive German parachute drops. After getting uniforms we were allowed into Richmond at the weekends, but had to be back in barracks by 10.00pm.

After four weeks we did our first route march in full kit. This was of 12 miles to Bellerby Moor, near Leyburn, for practice of firing all weapons and live grenade throwing. This took place over four days and was spent in a hutted camp. After was the march back to Richmond for the remainder of the eight-weeks initial training. Part of that time was spent guarding an emergency RAF landing ground which served as back-up for Catterick airfield - in case that was bombed out of action. In August, our training completed, we were split up to go to various units all over the country. The majority of us went south to join the 7th Battalion, which had sustained casualties at Dunkirk. The headquarters was at Wimborne, Dorset but a few of us went to D-company at Canford Cliffs and Sandbanks on the coast.

I was placed in a section of seven men, led by Lance Corporal Jim Mason. A year older than I, he was to become my life-long friend. Jim came from Horton-in-Ribblesdale near Settle and went to Skipton Grammar School - which used to play my school at rugby. 7th Battalion was formed as a territorial unit between the wars, with men mostly from the east and north-east coastal area.

All through that autumn there was a real threat of invasion and we occupied several large detached houses on Sandbanks beach - all the civilians having been evacuated from the coast. The same area is now regarded as millionaire's row and one of the world's most expensive property hot-spots. We dug trenches in the sandy beach and, with just one strand of barbed wire and no mines laid in front, we were expected to defeat any German assault with only light Bren machine guns and rifles. Luckily for us there was no invasion. Our dining hall was just down the road at the Haven Hotel, near the ferry that crosses over to Studland Heath. During Battle of Britain days in September I remember standing on guard armed with a tripod-mounted Bren gun, to fire at low-flying German aircraft. These came directly overhead every morning in their hundreds on their way to bomb London but never low enough to be reached with our small-arms fire. Many were shot down by the Spitfires and Hurricanes and we had good views of the dog-fights.

With the arrival of October the threat of invasion receded, the Germans failed to defeat the RAF and had lost large numbers of aircraft. They then put all their effort into trying to bomb London into submission. I experienced this when I was given my first leave on 15th October. I left Bournemouth by rail late in the evening and there were air-raid alerts all the way to London - the trains had to reduce their speed to 15 mph. I finally arrived in London at 6.00am the next morning - my seven days leave already reduced to six. It was necessary to step over sleeping people when descending into the tube at Waterloo. By Kings Cross I had joined several others heading for Leeds. It was 9.00am before we boarded the train - which was then not allowed to leave the station due to an air-raid alert. We were then ordered to get off and go down the tube until the all-clear sounded. I finally arrived home after a 22-hour journey - just in time to go and meet Nora from work.

Travelling was made all the more difficult by having to haul all our kit in two kit bags, equipment and side-arms, a rifle. With all the trains packed, it became something of a nightmare, making me feel like a pack mule!

I had to allow a day to get back which reduced my leave to five days. Nora's parents allowed me to stay with them to give us maximum time together but she wasn't allowed any time off work. We just had to make the best of it and in no time at all I was departing again. I had also received a letter which informed me the battalion had moved and ordered me to report to Castle Cary in Somerset.

I went via Bristol to Frome, where army transport was laid on to Castle Cary - our new 'home'. D-Company consisted of three platoons, 16, 17 and 18 - with about 30 men in each. I was in 18 and still in Jim Mason's section. The billet had been an old rope-works and had no heating except a ridiculously small stove, no internal water - only a long wooden trough outside with several cold taps. Behind this a toilet block covered with hessian. This was just one of the many hardships we had to face during the bitterly cold winter that followed. 7th Battalion was now part of the 69th Brigade of the famous 50th (Tyne-Tees) Division which had been badly mauled in France during the retreat to Dunkirk. This was now building back up to full strength, led by General (later Field Marshall) Montgomery who started an intensive six-month training programme. Besides local company training, route marches, PT and cross-country runs, there were divisional schemes, such as mock battles on Salisbury Plain and Exmoor.

On a lighter note, my platoon occupied the upper floor of the rope works in Castle Cary. We were on two-tier bunks and in charge was Corporal Brockless, an ex-butcher from Malton. What entertainment! There was an old gramophone with just two records, 'If you're Irish, come into the parlour', which was a good tune to sing on route marches, and 'Deep is the Night, Tristesse', which is still one of my favourite tunes. There was not much fun in going out at night in a blacked-out village but there was a small NAAFI for tea and cakes and a Toc-H canteen, where several of our own men provided entertainment. There was Al Hughes, a brilliant pianist, and Sergeant Simmons, a veteran from before the war with service in India, singing popular songs like, 'Music Maestro, Please'. We had church parade on Sunday mornings when not training. Jim and I would also go to evening service when possible.

Fig 7: D Company HQ, Castle Cary, May 1941.
Back row (left to right): Corporal Freddie Hindle, Joe Eastwood, John, Sid Cropper, Bill Kell and Tom Spruce. Front Row: Corporal Steve Andrews, Captain Kirkus, Major Scott, Sergeant Major Williams and CQMS Pat Lewis.

I should mention the food - breakfast was porridge and fatty bacon, corned beef, potatoes, rice and haversack sandwiches, cheese and corned beef. Cookhouse was a small lean-to shed, open along the front and the cooking done by two men not being particularly conscious of good hygiene methods!

In mid-December, seven-days' leave was started, one platoon at a time, so we were the last to go on 7th January. This was not such a hairy journey as the earlier London route but we still had to carry all our kit and equipment - which I think saved me injury when I fell heavily on Bristol's Temple Meads Station while running to catch a connection to Leeds. I felt sorry for Jim as he had

Fig 8: Castle Cary - May 1941

Back row (left to right) John, Wilf Young and Jim Mason

Front row: Sid Walker and Bill Grey

a further two-hour journey to Horton after I left him. I spent another few enjoyable days at home but Nora still had to work. This was now for the Air Ministry, who had taken over part of the Stonehouse Mill. I only had about five and a half days at home. It was soon back to Castle Cary and the 'delights' of doing 30 mile-a-day route marches - getting back on almost tip-toe due to blistered heels.

One particular divisional scheme stands out in my memory which lasted three days, one day of which we were purposely denied any food till evening - all part of Montgomery's 'toughening up programme'. We also had one night spent slogging it over Exmoor in bitter frosty weather. Being so high above sea-level we could see Swansea being heavily bombed - an awesome sight. The final day was spent on a mock attack by the whole Brigade on Barnstaple, supposedly held by the enemy. It had barely got started when a snowstorm began, so it was called off in very bad visibility and transport was called for. We got the ever reliable three-ton covered trucks but the East Yorkshires had several old buses, resulting in three men, sitting in the back of one being killed by fumes from a faulty exhaust.

About the middle of February found us involved in another of Montgomery's schemes - to slog it for 75-miles in three days over Salisbury Plain and the surrounding countryside. We had to try to find somewhere to sleep at night in the still bitterly cold weather. The second night several of us found a barn full of straw on the outskirts of a farm but during the night I became ill. I was seen by Corporal Brown, the Medical Officer's Assistant - who said my temperature was 104 degrees, I was rushed in the medical truck to a sick-bay which had been set up in an old school in Bruton, three miles from Castle Cary. I had got the 'flu and was still in a semi-conscious daze when the MO arrived back later in the day from the scheme. I clearly remember his exact words, "Give him a pill, Brown, he'll be all right". He was popularly known as Doc

Webster and was a gynaecology doctor in Bridlington before the war. When he came again a few days later my temperature had dropped to normal, so he said I could go home on seven days sick leave, which came as a marvellous surprise. I went back to Castle Cary to collect a rail warrant and ration cards and, as all my kit and equipment had been taken into storage when I was ill, I was allowed to leave it there, which made the journey home so much easier.

Nora was completely surprised when I walked in the same evening, and we had five very happy days. The day less represents the need to allow a day to travel back. The day before I got home Wakefield, Wrenthorpe and Leeds were bombed on the night of 14th March with several fatalities and many more casualties in Leeds. At the weekend we were able to go and see some of the damage in Leeds and do some shopping. Being engaged, we discussed when we might marry, especially as I could be going overseas in the near future. We didn't reach a definite decision before it was time for me to go back. My friend, Jim, had already married Margaret on his January leave and this had set me thinking that Nora and I should be doing the same.

I hadn't been long back at Castle Cary before we were told we would soon be going on embarkation leave. Before that, on 3rd April, we took part in a mock battle on Salisbury Plain, watched by King George VI with his escort of top brass and newsreel cameramen. Some of the film was shown with the news at the Playhouse while I was at home.

The following day all of us were sent home for seven days. We were not able to get away before evening and travelled overnight. I was knocking on the door of number 31 Hope Street at 6.00am on Saturday 5th April. After an urgent discussion Nora and I decided we would try to get married but didn't know if it would be possible in the short time available. After breakfast we went to see the St. John's vicar who seemed very reluctant, asking 'Why do you wish to get married so young?' - both of us were only 20 and this being wartime. He saw that we were determined and said he would marry us on the morning of Monday 7th - providing we had our parents' consent and a special licence was obtained. I was lucky in getting this at the register office - it being open on Saturday. I think it cost £3, which just about bankrupt me! I discovered Dad was working on an air-raid shelter in West Parade and he signed a parental consent form. I still needed this even though I was less than a week away from my 21st birthday, which was the youngest you could be to marry without consent. Nora had to shop for an outfit and had to use some of her mother's clothing coupons along with her own to buy a suitable costume and all the other necessities. In that respect I had no problem, as we were not allowed to wear civilian clothes even to get married!

The wedding was bound to be a very quiet affair, as hardly anyone was allowed time off work to attend. There were only Nora's parents, my sister Millie, and Nora's relations, Elsie and Mo Eyre, at whose house I had stayed the previous night. We were married in St. John's Church promptly at 11.00am on Monday 7th April 1941, with just a quiet celebration at home afterwards. Nora had to return to work the following day.

To make the journey back to Castle Cary, we had been ordered to report to a special troop train from York station, which was to leave at midnight on Thursday the 10th. Then came the moments we will never forget. A tearful parting on Westgate Station on a cold, frosty night with light snow falling. Neither of us knowing what the future held or even if we would ever survive to be together again.

I met up with Jim on the train, so we had plenty to talk about and, as the train pulled out my 21st birthday dawned - a dramatic start to any birthday!

Fig 9: John and Nora's wedding - 7th April 1941

Arriving the following morning we found all of 17 Platoon already back - all Lancashire lads transferred from South Lancashire Regiment. Instead of crossing to York they had gone straight down to Castle Cary. As they had been marked absent in York, they were all put on a charge - losing seven days pay. This was a typical nonsensical example of army regulations at that time.

This was Easter weekend - during which Bristol suffered a very heavy air raid and we were taken there on the Sunday morning to help where we could. I particularly remember seeing a young girl weeping by a massive hole which had been a pub run by her parents - both of who were killed. Some of us were set to work at the ruined tram depot now in danger of collapse. The steelwork had to be safely brought down using ladders, which was very precarious work.

After this came another four or five weeks training routine in much better weather and without Monty's gruelling schemes as he now had charge of all Southern Command. General Franklyn now commanded 50th Division.

Chapter 3

Around the middle of May '41 we were issued with tropical kit. This comprised of khaki drill shorts and shirt, calf-length stockings with the green regimental flash round the top, a mosquito net for protection at night and a light-weight topee headwear. The shorts had a long turn-up, to be turned down into longs when mosquitoes got troublesome. Although not a word was said about our destination, it was obviously the Middle East.

On 30th of May we were taken on the long train journey north to Gourock on the Clyde, where a large convoy of ships was assembling and we boarded HM troop ship 'Mooltan'. This turned out to really be a converted old Indian cargo boat, with a crew, and British merchant navy officers. 'D' Company was placed in a converted cargo hold, approached from the deck by three flights of wooden stairs. To say the accommodation was cramped would be an understatement. Long mess tables with overhead racks to store all our kit, equipment and weapons. Slung over-head were closely-packed hammocks, to be let down over the tables at night. Toilet facilities were three cubicles in one corner and the showers used sea-water. This all gave a hint of problems to come - the hot, fetid atmosphere was to be our home for the next five weeks - we didn't know this at the time, thankfully.

The ship was transporting the bulk of 69th Brigade - over 2,000 men - and should have sailed on the following day. Naval action in the Atlantic meant we didn't get underway until 3rd June. The

Fig 10: D Company 7th Battalion Green Howards May 1941. John is second from right of the kneeling men.

German battleship, 'Bismark', was being attacked by the Royal Navy and RAF as it tried to reach its home port of Brest. It was crippled and finally sank before reaching there.

An aside; before setting off on my war-time travels abroad, I would like to draw your attention to three maps located in the back pages of the book, these may give you a clearer picture of my journey.

On the first day out from port there were alarms and we had to rush on deck wearing lifebelts but no attack came. It was a very large well escorted convoy - the cruiser, HMS Birmingham, sailed alongside us. For the first few days a westerly direction was taken, before we sailed south. This route was taken in an attempt to avoid U-boat attacks. A menace of a different kind soon appeared with most of us afflicted with 'the runs' - though we were told it was just another form of sea-sickness. This ailment lasted several days, with no medication offered, causing constant queues at the three toilets. These would continually block and overflow onto the deck. Really bad cases were packed off to the sick-bay. Relief was felt by all when it finally subsided.

Then a routine was started - an after breakfast parade on top deck for ship's morning rounds, lifebelts worn and a separate item of kit inspection every day. This would cause chaos on the mess table as random items were selected each of which would inevitably be at the bottom of the kit bag. Then there would be a limited amount of training. With deck space limited we were restricted to simple exercises and lectures on all things army related.

After sailing out towards America the convoy turned south and day-by-day the weather got warmer, allowing us to wear our tropical kit. On some nights we were allowed to take our single blanket and sleep on deck. I never did get used to the hammock - being unable to sleep when on my back.

Three weeks from leaving the Clyde, we docked for two days at Freetown, West Africa, for re-fuelling and taking on stores. We were not allowed on shore but I couldn't have done it anyway as I went down with 'flu-like symptoms again in over 100 degree (Fahrenheit) temperatures and spent a time in sick bay being sponged down. We got on our way again - with the Cape of Good Hope ahead. The reason for needing to sail all the way around Africa was that the Mediterranean Sea was virtually a 'no-go' area. This was due to it being dominated by the German and Italian navies, who had been causing unacceptable numbers of sinkings. We finally arrived at Durban, on Africa's south-east coast, and were really happy to say goodbye to 'Mooltan'.

We were soon on a train to Clairwood race course, just a few miles from the docks. A tented camp had been set up here to give troops in transit to Egypt and the Far East a welcome break. This gave us a week's leave, free from any parades or duties and included plenty of un-rationed food, no blackout and the camp being brilliantly lit all night. Although in the middle of the southern hemisphere winter we had warm, sunny days. We were given some pay which allowed us to take the train into Durban every day to enjoy very good cheap meals and take part in relaxing games. We also attended cinemas open to the night sky as we did not need to return to camp until midnight, giving some compensation for the weeks spent on Mooltan!

All too soon it was back to the docks and wonder of wonders, to board the cruise ship 'Mauritania' which, along with several other famous cruise liners, had been converted to troop carriers. I remember seeing HMS Barham, one of Britain's greatest battleships, in dry dock for a refit. Tragically, after joining the Mediterranean fleet, it was sunk a few months later. The unescorted convoy set sail for Egypt, with two other liners. These were the Dutch 'Nieu Amsterdam' and the French 'Ile de

France'. They were all (with a fast 35-knots speed) able to show a clean pair of heels to any prowling 'U' boat. The total number of troops being transported would be between eight and nine thousand - almost the entire 50th Division. In complete contrast to the 'Mooltan' the accommodation comprised four of us to a twin-bunk stateroom. Two extra bunks were installed but there was still plenty of space for four. Best of all we were on one of the upper decks. I had a porthole just above my bunk, to watch the other two great ships racing along - a magnificent sight.

With so many men to feed, there were three sittings on spotlessly laid out tables - white tablecloths, the ship's cutlery, bowls of unrationed sugar and as much good South African food as we could eat. Absolute bliss, but after ten days and like all good things, it came to an end. Having sailed right up the Indian Ocean and seeing no sign of enemy action, we sailed into Port Tufiqh at the southern end of the Suez Canal. The next stage of our journey was by bumpy three-ton army trucks to a desert camp at Quassasin, near Ismailia. This was back to reality with a vengeance! Over a hundred degree heat and tents full of flies! The only consolation was there was very little training to do in the fierce heat - only night guarding. By the time we arrived at Tufiqh it had been seven weeks since we left Scotland.

At that time the Desert War was more or less static, having see-sawed since it began over a year earlier. This had been between the Egyptian border and hundreds of miles to the west at El Agheila and Benghazi. We thought our next move would be up to the front to take part in another advance but this was not so.

After three weeks at Quassasin and without being told anything in advance, we were transported to Port Said. Here we boarded the British cruiser, HMS Neptune. Like HMS Barham this was also sunk in the 'Med' three months later. Only once aboard were we told we were heading for Cyprus. The whole deck area was crowded with troops, equipment and stores. I squatted under one of the gun barrels for the whole of the eight-hour crossing.

The ship berthed shortly after midnight in bright moonlight but still managed to collide with an old wooden pier, demolishing it. This was Famagusta harbour and we spent the remainder of the night on a nearby beach. The next day we were told our role was to prepare the island's defences - mainly digging trenches. The Germans had already taken Greece and Crete and it was expected Cyprus would be the next target. After being taken to Larnaca and spending a few fairly easy days, we went on to Limassol. There, just inland in a wooded area, it was back to trench digging in hard, stony ground and causing me a very painful knee injury. The treatment for this being a kind of poultice, containing some horrible black stuff which, after a few days' rest, eased the pain and swelling. I went back to duty but this periodically gave me trouble over the next three and a half years, until a cystic cartilage was removed.

Before leaving England I had been given the job of Company runner, joining the small HQ of two officers and about six other men. Officially I had to convey messages from our Commanding Officer, Major Scott, to all three platoon officers but it wasn't at all hectic until we saw action.

The second-in-command, Captain Kirkus was sent to run a small leave camp in the Troodos Mountains and took me with him. Kirkus was a sales rep. from Hornsea before the war - working for a British oil and cake company which supplied farmers with animal food. My role was just to serve the officer's meals from the small cookhouse and also drinks in the evening. In case you're wondering - I did get drunk, but only once. The cook had to put me to bed and next morning it was 'never again' time! He had already seen action in the desert with the 11th Hussars, an armoured car regiment and had a lot of stories to tell.

Apart from scalding my foot (which laid me up for a day or two) the only other thing to mention about Troodos was the lovely cool weather - coming as it did after the heat at sea level. When the camp was closed in October, we pulled out in a snowstorm wearing our greatcoats. These were soon discarded when we got back to the heat.

I have a short memory block when all I remember is being in a tented hospital (No. 17) – which was a casualty clearing station based in the capital, Nicosia. I don't recall the reason for this but early in November, I was discharged back to unit as another move was imminent.

On 16th November we sailed from Famagusta on the destroyer, HMS Kingston which tragically, like HMS Barham and HMS Neptune, was also later sunk. Our next destination was Palestine - docking at Haifa on the 17th. We were then transported by coast road north, stopping near a pre-war barracks named Sidney Smith's. We camped just inland in an orange grove and, yes, the Jaffa oranges were luscious! Then came two more weeks of training in the still hot weather with 20 or more miles-a-day route marches.

On 1st December we started off in convoy on a thousand mile journey, first passing into what was then known as Trans-Jordan. We followed an oil pipeline which went all the way from northern Iraq to the terminal at Haifa. Each night we camped in open desert. Iraq had been under British rule since the First World War - when it was part of what was known as Mesopotamia. By 1941 Germany had joined the Desert War. Hitler had ambitions to control the whole Middle East and its massive oil fields and so backed an Arab revolt. This was led by one Rashid Ali who was supplied with aircraft to try and eliminate the only permanent RAF base at Habbaniya in the central desert region. By then the

Fig 11: Telegram to Nora - sent from Palestine

9th Australian division, which had already seen action in Libya, was quickly transferred to Iraq. They soon put down the revolt after a battle at Habbaniya. We of the 50th Division were sent to relieve the Aussies who went back into Libya.

Our destination was the far north at Kirkuk oil field. The Germans had attacked Russia in June and advanced so quickly that they were already threatening to break through the Caucasus Mountains to the oil fields. On the way were several Air Force landing grounds where we camped for the night. One of them was near Baghdad which found us driving through in a closed up convoy in case of trouble. The only other inhabited region we passed through apart from Habbaniya (where we spent one night) was our final destination of Kirkuk. We got here after a week of following mostly bumpy desert tracks - occasionally passing small Arab encampments and being greeted by packs of howling dogs who would race after the convoy. Kirkuk brought to an end our thousand miles following the pipeline.

Having driven beyond the town for a mile or two, we were directed on to an area which was nothing more than a ploughed field. This was just off the main road to Mosul, the most northerly town leading to the Caucasus. By then it was quite dark and raining heavily as we set about erecting our square eight-man tents. What a shambles this turned out to be! There was no solid earth in which to drive the pegs – which was made worse by the wet conditions and working in semi-darkness. We did manage it in a fashion and tried to settle down for the night. It was not to be! Not long after the whole tent collapsed on top of us. What a miserable night that was. The rain aside; it was at the start of the northern Iraq winter and bitterly cold.

So, at the start of several thoroughly miserable weeks, a training programme was started. We experienced several severe overnight frosts, which at least hardened up the camping ground – after our sloshing about on the rain-soaked ground. The ground being now harder we had managed to dig the tents in - to about two feet below ground level. I still don't know how we all survived the terrible cold of those December weeks, typically having to sleep fully clothed.

I have a very clear memory of Christmas Day 1941. It was army tradition that Christmas dinner be served by officers to all other ranks. This was achieved by digging two foot deep trenches in a box shape, about 12-yards square. The company were sitting facing inwards with our legs dangling in the trench. All the food was brought in and served in the finest tradition by the officers. I don't remember what we ate but it had to be cooked in the open-air field kitchen.

Three more weeks went by and we got orders to pack up and prepare to move again, but once more we had no hint of our destination. We assumed that this time it would be to the Libyan desert. After a long trek south, passing back through Jordan, we found ourselves settling in much warmer temperatures. We were in a tented camp next door to a Jewish settlement, a kibbutz called Rosch Pinna. This was in the Galilee area, with not a lot to do for the next week or so but get the horrible cold of northern Iraq out of our system. This was 22nd January '42.

You must, by now, be wondering how I can remember all these precise details. I am fortunate in that I kept and retained a small diary with a list of dates of my wartime movements.

Back in Palestine - which became part of Isreal in 1948 - no sooner had we settled in the pleasant surroundings of Rosch Pinna, than orders came to pack up and move on, which made us begin to feel like the desert nomads! On 30th January we headed north into Syria, passing through the ancient ruins of Baalbec, into a mountainous region - now called the Golan Heights. We found ourselves at an isolated hutted camp, which had recently been vacated by the 9th Australians, who had returned to the Desert War. We were there for mountain training and a leave rota was started for Beirut, but within a day or two of going myself, it was all cancelled.

At this time, following a spectacular advance by our army to El Agheila, beyond Benghazi, they were again being pushed back by Rommel's forces and were in urgent need of reinforcements - which meant us of the 50th Division. February 15th found us heading south through Beirut to join the main road going south into Egypt. At least I got to see the town, I think in a state much better then than with the present day troubles in that region.

We went down the Lebanon coast - into Palestine, through Haifa, what is now known as the Gaza Strip and across the border into Egypt and into the Sinai Desert. By 17th February we were across the Suez Canal and headed for Cairo. There was no stopping to sample that city's 'dubious delights' - driving through the centre in closed up convoy. One thing I remember seeing is a huge roadside poster, advertising the latest Hollywood blockbuster film, 'Blood and Sand', starring Tyrone Power. Surprisingly it was not about the Desert War, but bull fighting. Nevertheless it seemed very topical!

I mentioned earlier about the army's withdrawal from El Agheila and Benghazi in January and early February. They had managed to hold the Germans at an old defensive line at Ein El Gazala, 20-miles along the coast road west from Tobruk. The line of defensive positions stretching south into the desert for 20-miles to Bir Hacheim, a French Foreign Legion outpost before the war. I'm not certain about the distance but I think we were now around four hundred miles west of Cairo. The estimate is based on a full two-day trek since leaving the city. We arrived on the afternoon of February 20th.

Now, I must explain that the line was a series of fortified boxes with minefields in front, infantry and some artillery in the box and armoured units to the rear. In the Gazala coastal, was the 1st South African division box, then the Durham Light infantry of 151 brigade (50th Division) then 150 Brigade, 4th East

Yorkshire and 4th and 5th Green Howards, then our 69th, 5th East Yorkshire, 6th and 7th Green Howards, and finally at Bir Hacheim, the Free French Brigade (mostly Foreign Legion).

We were taking over the positions from the 51st Highland Division, the Cameronians, who had helped to hold the Germans after the withdrawal from Benghazi. There was a good system of trenches and dug-outs which proved lucky for us. We were trying to sort ourselves out after leaving the transport when, seeming to appear from nowhere, three Messerschmitt fighters dived on us, machine gunning. My friend, Freddie Hindle (who was another member of Company HQ) and I dived into the nearest trench with our sergeant-major landing on top of us, the bullets stirring up the sandy ground. Luckily, at least in the immediate area, no one was wounded. And so ended our baptism of fire.

Most of our kit had been left behind at base in Cairo, so we only had the bare essentials - a blanket and weapons. Food was nearly all tinned, corned beef, fatty bacon, Machonache stew (a name familiar to First World War troops), hard tack biscuits, rice and, very rarely, tinned fruit. Water was the everlasting problem throughout the Desert War Campaign. This was brought up to the front in flimsy square two-gallon tins over bumpy desert tracks. Some would leak at the seams and arrive half empty, causing strict rationing of two pints per man for all purposes. There was a small quantity of well water for washing but this was unfit for drinking. The very warm daytime temperature rose to over 100 degrees by the summer which meant we were constantly thirsty.

The sun going down would bring welcome relief but not from thirst except on one night when it actually rained. Freddie and I, in our shared dug-out woke up wet through. Some nights were spent on guard duty - the usual two hours on and four off and always at dawn and dusk everyone 'stood to' as these times were judged most likely for an enemy attack.

The three months following our arrival was something of a stalemate, with both sides reluctant to mount a full scale attack. Instead we were both building up strength, especially in tanks and guns. In the meantime, mobile columns of infantry and artillery were sent out through the minefield, into the several miles of desert no-man's land.

Malta was heavily bombed from two airfields, Tmimi and Mechili in March. These were in the coastal area of the German line and we joined one of the mobile columns to attack them. Advancing on foot, after our transport went back out of range of the shelling we soon came under shellfire. This was coming from a German column, sheltering behind rising ground about a mile away. I was walking alongside Syd Cropper, our signaller with an 'Eighteen' wireless set strapped on his back. He was receiving messages from Battalion HQ for our company officers, which I had to deliver by word of mouth to our three platoon officers. Syd received a shell fragment through the neck and fell dead. I had to dash round our still advancing platoon officers to tell them what had happened.

Eventually a halt was called to the advance - we were told to 'dig in' for the night. We always carried an entrenching tool, which was a small spade with a short handle. It was useless in the hard stony ground of the Libyan Desert - which wasn't the anticipated sand. The shelling got heavier towards dusk, which caused several casualties. When, with the darkness it ceased, I was detailed to escort several walking wounded to the regimental aid post, half a mile to the rear. This led to a very uncomfortable night - trying to keep alert for a possible night attack, which never came. With daylight and no explanation, we were suddenly ordered to withdraw back to our positions in the brigade box.

Transport was hurriedly called up, with the drivers not even giving us enough time to jump on before setting off - resulting in a good number being left to be taken prisoner or worse. I ran alongside a truck already gathering speed and first flinging my rifle on, managed to cling on to the open truck side and climb up. I saw one of my mates from Richmond days, Dennis Walsh, clamber on the back of another truck, only to fall off backwards - he was never seen again.

After this disastrous episode things became quiet for a while. So much that we were driven to the coast, one truckload at a time, for a welcome wash in the sea. Being driven back in one of the many dust storms meant we were dirtier than when we set out! I was put on a waiting list to go back on a driving course, but future events dictated otherwise.

April brought really hot weather with flies settling on all the food. A mug of tea would be black with them. A tin of corned beef would run out in a gooey mess, tasting saltier still – which would only aggravate our thirst. We would get a pint in our water bottle in the morning to last the whole day, which required tremendous will power to resist drinking the lot at one go. A few men even took to drinking their own urine, with disastrous results. Then a few would do anything to get returned to base, L.O.B. (left out of battle). One genuine case was Major Scott, our Company Commanding Officer and a veteran of the First World War. He was sent home with rheumatic fever. Our bully of a sergeant major went sick with a stomach problem, not missed by anyone along with a corporal who became a nervous wreck and a platoon lieutenant who shot himself in the foot - a court-martial offence.

In Tobruk, about 20-miles to our rear, was a bulk NAAFI store, supplying the whole 8th Army with rationed chocolate, cigarettes and other essentials like toothpaste and soap. After Major Scott's departure Captain Kirkus was made Company Commander. I was detailed to accompany him and our 15cwt. open-truck driver, 'Rocky' Rayner, to Tobruk. However, at the last minute I was put on some other duty. On the way the truck was attacked by a common shell firing Messerschmitt 110. The captain, who had followed the correct procedure and ran away was hit by a shell which severed his leg. Rocky, who had dived under the truck, emerged unscathed. We lost him later when he left us to become driver for General Maitland-Wilson, Commander-in-Chief of all the Middle East Forces. I didn't see Captain Kirkus again, but got a nice letter from him after the war, wishing my wife and I well and saying he was able to resume his pre-war job.

After Captain Kirkus was wounded our next Commanding Officer (C.O.) was Captain Swift - who came from another company. He only lasted a few weeks before he was killed in the Cauldron battles. Captain Jackson replaced him as the fourth C.O. in just a few weeks until - staying with us until he was taken prisoner.

All through April and well into May we were expecting to take part in a new offensive, but Rommel made the first move on 26th May, by advancing first south, skirting around the Free French Brigade and then attacking them in the rear with all his armoured force. His 15th and 21st Panzer Divisions had been fully reinforced, against which the British armour was proved to be incapable of defeating. Our tank strength of Matildas, Valentines, Honeys and Stuarts, with nothing heavier than a two pounder gun were no match for the German Mark IV's and their 88mm guns. These were also used to shell our positions. American General Grant tanks eventually appeared on the battlefield, but too few to affect the outcome of the Gazala battles. The French put up a heroic defence but, after two weeks were over-run and suffered many casualties. Why our armour was never fully used in an all-out assault – instead being sent in small units - was never fully explained. This caused much controversy and the later sackings of some commanders.

Meanwhile we were left sitting in our box being shelled and bombed daily. 150 Brigade Box was attacked, the 5th Green Howards being virtually wiped out and the Germans broke through to their forces in our rear. Rommel's aim was to head north and cut off the coast road but the final battle of the whole Gazala line was about to begin. This determined whether the 8th Army advanced or once again retreated to the next prepared position inside the Egyptian frontier. The area behind our Brigade box became known as 'The Cauldron', where Rommel inflicted severe losses on our tanks and infantry.

In the middle of June our whole 7th Battalion started advancing at dawn behind a screen of tanks, our job being to subdue German infantry accompanying their armour. Our new company commander, Captain Swift, was killed early in the battle and was replaced by Captain Jackson, who was a solicitor from Bridlington before the war and a true gentleman to boot. I went in on our HQ truck, still being driven by Rocky Rainer, with Freddie Hindle, Joe Eastwood and Bill Kell. We immediately came under heavy fire from the dreaded 88mm guns and were ordered to dig-in behind the vehicle, an impossible task in the hard stony ground. How we wished it had been the classic desert sand!

Meanwhile the whole battalion was taking unacceptable losses, later it was found that out of a total battalion strength of 800 men, we had lost 300 in just a 90-minute period - killed, wounded or taken as prisoners. Captain Jackson was soon racing round the vehicles, shouting at us to turn and quickly make our way back to the Brigade box - an order we obeyed with alacrity! Later that day we learned that the whole Gazala line was to be evacuated as the army commander, General Ritchie did not wish to lose any more infantry units. He was later sacked for failure to defeat the Germans. The plan was to break out that same night, with transport well spaced out and race south through the

German lines in bright moonlight for several miles before turning east to try to reach the frontier position, where it was planned to make a stand.

In the previous weeks, a large bulk supply of boxed and tinned food had been built up, and we were told to destroy as much as possible. A large amount was still left, after we had piled as much as possible on the truck. When darkness fell, it was found that the bright moonlight, reflecting on the windscreens, was attracting enemy fire. What was left of the battalion after the 'Cauldron Battle' was drawn up on transport, well spaced out, waiting for the order to make a dash through the enemy supply lines. Our sergeant-major, Pat Lewis, dashed round smashing windscreens, trying to lessen the shell fire, though this didn't achieve much.

When the order to move off came we made good progress, until our truck hit a patch of soft sand and sank almost axle deep. This was deeply unlucky because the area was mostly firm ground. The four of us must have struggled for a half-hour, but finally got it clear, when we were aware that several other trucks were turning round and heading north for the coast road, so we promptly joined them. By this time, dawn was breaking, and the small convoy was joined by a troop of 25-pound artillery, also making for the coast with orders to proceed into the Tobruk perimeter. As we got nearer to the road, we met several small groups of South Africans, who told us that their division had already gone into Tobruk. They had been left as rearguard for stragglers like us, in case of possible attack from the west.

Here I must mention my friend, Jim Mason, who had gone with the group breaking out south. Just before the 'Cauldron Battle', D Company had been issued with 8.2-pound anti-tank guns mounted on a portee. This was simply a mobile platform, with a gun-shield and a two-man crew. They were sent against the Mark-IV 88s and never stood a chance. Seven were soon knocked out, the crews either killed or made prisoner. Jim's gun was the only one to survive but not without incident. A shell passed straight through the middle of the shield and within inches of Jim's head and that of his number two, 'Smudger' Smith. I saw evidence of this miracle after the withdrawal.

Back to the coast road - of which we were within sight, when suddenly we came under shellfire. This was coming from the first of Rommel's advancing columns. Our heroic troop of gunners gave answering fire, allowing our whole column to race down to Tobruk. Once there we learned it was to be held under siege, as in the year before. What was left of the 8th Army was racing for the Egyptian frontier, to make a stand. We passed through the town on 19th June.

General Klopper, then commander, surrendered the town on 21st June - against all orders, with enemy forces already attacking the outer perimeter defences. To surrender without a fight, with almost the whole division of around 9,000 men intact and taken prisoner which caused outrage at home. To make matters worse, when Churchill received the news, he was in the mid-Atlantic on an American warship, in conference with Roosevelt. With much reluctance he was obliged to tell the President, who was doing his utmost to help by supplying us with tanks, guns and many other items of war.

It was about this time that our column reached the frontier - to learn that the line was not going to be held. Orders were that the remnants of the army was to fall back much further to the last fortified position before the Nile Delta at El Alamein. This decision caused much panic in the base areas. All secret documents were destroyed and preparation was made to evacuate further up the Nile.

At this time the 8th Army commander, General Ritchie, was sacked. Brigadier 'Strafer' Gott replaced him for a short while until he was killed in an air crash. The commander-in-chief of the Middle East Forces, Sir Claude Auchinlech, took charge for a short while before he was appointed commander-in-chief in India. It was after this that Churchill then sent General Montgomery out to take charge.

This however was all in the near future as we hurried on beyond the frontier, being harassed by the Stuka dive bombers, with their weird shrieking sirens wailing as they attacked. We finally stopped about 12-miles south into the desert from Mersa Matruh - then only a name on the map of the coastal area. I was about to jump off our truck when a Stuka started his dive, obviously aiming at us, but the bomb fell well away, injuring no one.

The remainder of the battalion was already in position after breaking through south from Gazala but many had been taken prisoner. Only around 300 of us remained, still commanded by Colonel McDonnell. He told us we were to stand as a delaying action to allow time for the re-enforcements from throughout Middle East Command to be brought up to the Alamein position for a final battle for the Delta.

The remnants of 50th Division was strung out up to the coast road at Matruh, which was held by 4th Indian Division (Ghurkhas and Sikhs). We had no heavy weapons left in the battalion, just one small two-inch mortar, which fired a small bomb, and our rifles. The prospects looked very bleak - this was 27th June.

Jim Mason had got through with the other column, so we were able to compare experiences since the 'Cauldron Battle.' Everyone was in a pretty sorry state by now, having not slept properly for over a month and on some nights not at all. This was the situation as the battalion took up position round the edges of a wahdi (a slight depression in the desert floor, possibly 100 yards long by 50 wide) affording us some protection from incoming assault.

The 28th passed quietly, giving us some respite but towards dusk German infantry were observed leaving their transport, obviously ready to mount an attack. It was 1.00am on the 29th when we heard the ominous rattle made by a tank's tracks. It suddenly appeared at the open end of the wahdi. Captain Towle of B-Company started firing the mortar, but with no success. Immediately the tank started blazing away, the first shell hitting a 15 cwt. truck, with the driver, Eric Major, still sitting in it. I'll never forget his agonising screams as it exploded in an instant fireball. Eric had been a member of a well-known Flamborough family of fishermen and lifeboat crew. I had first met him at Richmond during recruiting days, when we stood together on parade – by virtue of alphabetical order.

Within seconds, Colonel McDonnell walked towards the tank waving something white in surrender. He realised we had nothing to deal with the tank and decided to save further bloodshed. Although there was no moon, the brilliant night sky gave sufficient light for the enemy infantry following up behind the tank, to quickly round us up with shouts of "Hande Hoch. Hands up, Tommy". Freddie Hindle was a bit slow doing so and received a kick up the backside from a pocket-sized German brandishing a Spandau machine gun. Three men managed to escape, being a little distance from the rest, and fled into the desert. They were lucky to meet with another small column and all safely reached El Alamein. This was told to me much later in the war by Jim Mason, who was one of the three.

Chapter 4

We were guarded until daylight and lined-up ready to march to the coast, when an open German battle wagon drew up. General Rommel, who had the reputation of leading from the front, stood observing us. He must have thought what a sorry looking bunch we looked - filthy, unshaven and bleary-eyed through lack of sleep. The march to the coast in the intense heat, with no water offered, was sheer torture. We finally collapsed exhausted at the side of the coast road in the late afternoon awaiting transport westwards. Truckloads of Italian infantry passed, jeering at us, shouting, "Cairo, Cairo", convinced they would soon be there. Towards evening we were given a little water - but no food.

Although I now remember more Italian transport coming, I have no memory of the journey, which possibly lasted two days. We halted on the escarpment, a high plateau overlooking Tobruk harbour. Here a large temporary barbed-wire enclosure had been hastily erected and already contained several hundred prisoners - a fraction of the 80,000 taken by the Rome-Berlin Axis partnership since 26th May - by far the greater number from the Tobruk surrender.

Another memory lapse occurs now - for several days we squatted in the boiling sun with no sanitary arrangements. I think the food we were given was the Italian version of corned beef. This was horrible black-looking stuff along with rock-hard four-inch square biscuits. We must have been given water but the lack of this was always a problem. Numbers were meanwhile diminishing daily with groups being marched down to the harbour - presumably to be transported further west by sea. In the meantime we were able to watch the night-time bombing of the harbour by the RAF

The reader could be forgiven for thinking the 8th Army was a total shambles, losing the Gazala battles and retreating several hundred miles in the space of a few weeks. After the defeat there was really no choice but to fall back on the next prepared defence line at El Alamein and await the arrival of substantial reinforcements. The main problem since the Germans entered the Desert War was the superior fire power of the Africa Korps' 15th and 21st Panzer divisions and a lack of firm leadership in the higher echelons of command. This was rectified by the arrival of General Montgomery at El Alamein, and Churchill being successful in procuring armaments and planes from the Americans. This would finally turn the tide - the 8th Army didn't lose another battle.

Since leaving Gazala our small group of Company HQ had managed to stay together. We remained so when our turn came to descend to the harbour (along with around fifty others). We were put onto what proved to be an ancient German coal boat, with no facilities for passengers. We were given the usual tin of black corned beef, three biscuits and, with instructions to make it last two days, a little water. We were also told we must just sit or lie on top of the coal. The Lord alone knows what we must have looked like on reaching Benghazi harbour after hugging the coastline all the way. We were filthy and our shorts and shirts had been crawling with lice since we occupied the Gazala defences originally dug by the Italians.

On going ashore, it was soon obvious that the enemy had no organised way of dealing with thousands of prisoners. Another vast barbed-wire enclosure awaited us already containing thousands waiting to be moved on. Sanitary arrangements were totally inadequate. Several large deep pits had been dug in the sandy soil for use as latrines, with boards laid across on which to squat. Dysentery was already rife and soon the pits were overflowing - making it necessary to be always on the move trying to find a dry spot. Three of us managed to stay together - myself, Freddie Hindle and Laurie Addison from Sledmere, near Malton. Before the war Laurie had been a groom for Sir Richard Sykes at Sledmere House, who in turn had been one of our Battalion Officers in England but didn't go overseas. We spent three weeks in that horrible place, enduring the intense July heat, the misery of upset stomachs, very little food or water, flies and mosquitoes. I think if we had been kept there much longer, many would not have survived as the Italians provided little in the way of medical help.

On or about 28th July the three of us were in a group of about 50, being marched down to the docks and halted at the side of an Italian cargo vessel. As we filed over the gangplank, a German officer, presumably supervising the boarding, stood at the end saying, "My word, you lads need a shave!" In faultless English he continued; "I was educated at your Oxford University you know - good luck!" We could have said we needed a lot more than a shave! He also said, "Did you enjoy your Cook's tour of the Middle East?" This indicated they had known every move of 50th Division, making a mockery of the supposed tight security.

On deck we were again issued with the three day ration - a small tin of bully and three 'hard as concrete' biscuits. Then we were taken to a three foot square trap door in the deck which opened to reveal a vertical iron ladder. This lead down to the floor of the empty cargo hold, 10 to 12 feet below. They were obviously using boats like this to supply the Desert Army and then transporting the thousands of prisoners on the return voyage to the Italian mainland. A guard with a fixed bayonet stood motioning us to descend into the hold in semi-darkness, with just one small light.

So began another three-day nightmare journey. Almost immediately the toilet problem raised its ugly head, there being no facility in the hold. Makeshift toilets had been erected on deck to discharge into the sea. The trouble was the guards would only allow two men at a time to ascend, get relief and descend before more were allowed up. This inevitably resulted in some having to get relief literally where they stood. This led to most of us having permanent 'runs' caused, we were sure, by eating the horrible smelly black corned beef. It was either that or starve to death.

Thankfully no one died and, on 1st August, we were docked safely in Brindisi harbour on the south-east coast. We then marched or staggered to another barbed-wire enclosure some distance from the docks and watched by dozens of civilians at the roadside. These people were throwing tomatoes at their 'defeated' enemy - some we managed to catch and eat which only caused the usual problem later. Behind the wire we were given water but no food.

After several hours we were again on the move, the group now considerably enlarged with more PoWs arriving. What we didn't know until much later was that another boat had been sunk on the way over, possibly by aircraft operating from Malta, or torpedoed. There were no known survivors - at least we had been spared that ordeal.

The tomatoes soon took the inevitable effect on empty stomachs and many of us had no choice but to drop out to the roadside and find relief in the gutter - in a street full of people! What a humiliation this was - it had to be the nadir of our morale. After the headlong retreat of 8th Army from Gazala, the misery of being taken prisoner, with our bodies much weakened and being in filthy conditions for the whole of July, we had really reached rock bottom. Most definitely not 'stiff-upper-lip, we're British'.

We staggered at nightfall into Brindisi Railway Station to see a cattle-truck train awaiting. We were crammed into the trucks, not knowing where we were going. It was some relief to get the cool night air through the open sliding door. Several of us, me included, were still affected with the 'runs' and I remember through the night our two guards allowing to hang over the truck side, clinging on to a central bar across the opening, thereby getting blissful relief!

We knew we were travelling northwards up the Adriatic coast and eventually arrived in daylight at Bari. We were marched to what proved to be a recently established transit camp and we started to be given more humanitarian treatment. First a 200-gram, small brown loaf, acorn substitute black coffee and, heavenly, crystal-clear water, straight from the Appenines. A team of barbers shaved our heads before we moved on to some makeshift showers even the cold water didn't stop this being welcome, being the first full body wash for over five months. The only snag was we still had to wear our filthy shirt and shorts, having vainly tried to wash them in cold water and a piece of Italian soap from which it was almost impossible to get lather.

When finally allowed to walk about the camp - in the still hot sunshine - I approached a wire fence which separated us from some officers. Among these I spotted Captain Jackson. Upon seeing me, he came over to the fence, accompanied by Bill Bowes (the famous Yorkshire and England fast bowler - an artillery officer captured in the Gazala Battle.) Captain Jackson, seeing my shaved head and weakened appearance said, "Good Lord, John, what have they done to you?" They had been treated a bit better than us and a day or two later were sent off by air to Germany. We were left to sleep in small two-man bivouacs.

Later that day a kind of vegetable stew was served containing tiny bits of cheese and pasta and served again in the evening. After several days, during which I began to feel better, we again moved on back to the railway station, boarded the cattle trucks and travelled again through the night. The next morning we arrived at the Adriatic town of Porto-St-Georgio. Then, having been transferred to a small mountain railway, we travelled several miles up into the Appenines to the hill village, Monturano.

Here a large camp was still being constructed, which would eventually house 9,000 prisoners and was named Camp 70. These camps were mostly spread right across the southern half of the country. Once through the gates we came to a huge barn-like building which was already partly occupied. Entry to this was through three sets of double wooden doors. 16 sets of three-tier bunks in rows spread across the building with a single yard-wide access between rows. This building housed a total of 600 men.

One man, usually a sergeant, was put in charge of each row, for bread distribution and enforcing discipline. For my row it was Jock Thompson, he was always strict but scrupulously fair, which was needed in the cramped conditions where tension was always present. The day started at 6.15am with a stampede to the cookhouse for a mug of acorn coffee and one 250 gram piece of bread (to last all day). At midday we got a mug of thick soup (which was not as good as at Bari). At 6pm we received more soup and coffee. This was nothing more than a starvation diet.

We remained on this until two or three months later when Red Cross parcels started to arrive. Issued every fortnight, these parcels were either of British or Canadian origin, with one parcel to share between two. These would typically contain tinned food, plain biscuits, dried milk and tea. The two-week gap did not always apply, sometimes stretching to four or five weeks, but I'm sure it was the difference between life and death. Tea was brewed outside in empty milk tins over a fire of bits of wood scrounged from the Italians.

Now to the toilet and washing facilities - remember I wrote about the Benghazi facilities? Well, they must have sent their plans over to Monturano, because they were exact replicas. A half-dozen deep pits, with squat planks laid over. The only difference here was the huge camp area was about a quarter of a mile square, with the 'toilets' at the furthest extremity. These were well away from our abode but soon became infested with flies in the still very warm weather. For ablutions a long narrow building was near completion, with a trough running along the whole of one side at wash-basin height. This had a perforated pipe above which gave a constant stream of cold water. This would allow about 30 men to stand close together. As this was actually for 600 men it proved totally inadequate. I never saw a drop of hot water during the nine months I was there.

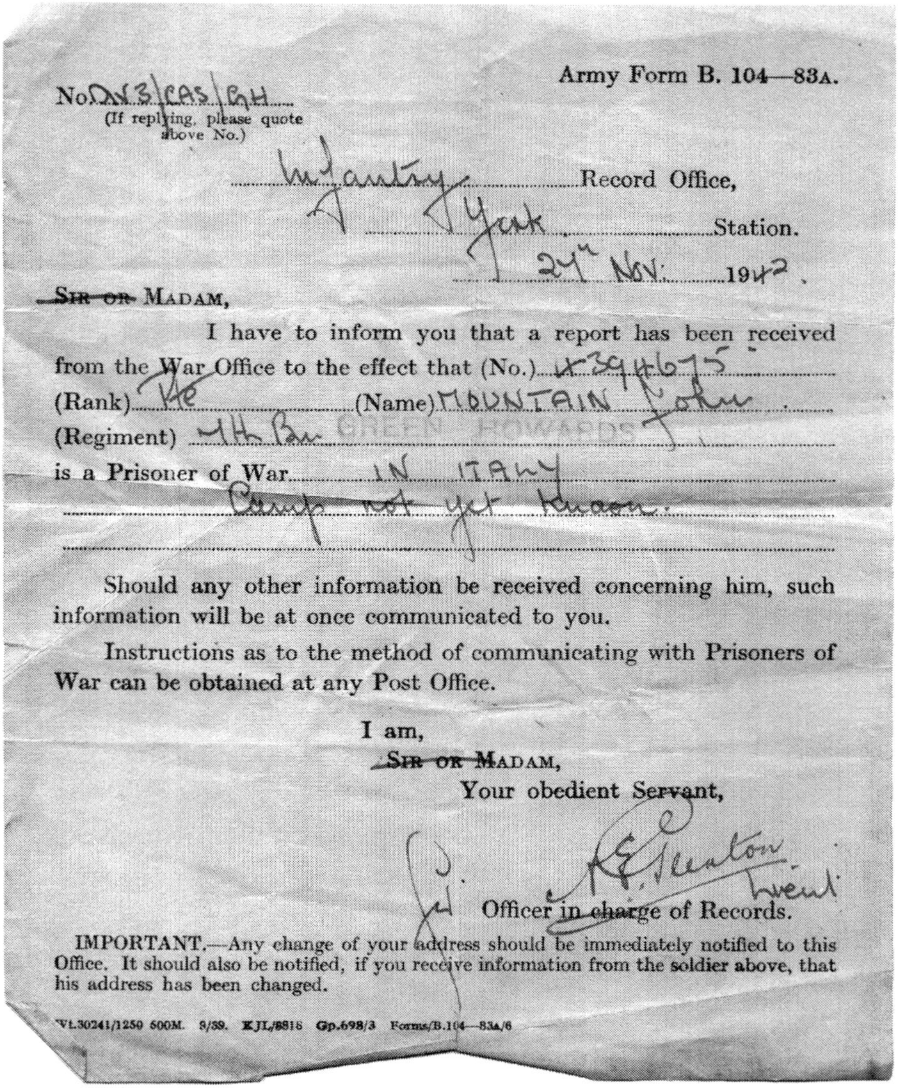

No. *[handwritten]* N.3/CAS/GH
(If replying, please quote above No.)

Army Form B. 104—83A.

[handwritten] Infantry .... Record Office,

[handwritten] York .... Station.

[handwritten] 24th Nov. ......19 42 .

Sir or Madam,

I have to inform you that a report has been received from the War Office to the effect that (No.) *[handwritten]* 4394675

(Rank) *[handwritten]* Pte. (Name) *[handwritten]* MOUNTAIN John

(Regiment) *[handwritten]* 4th Bn. Green Howards

is a Prisoner of War *[handwritten]* IN ITALY

[handwritten] Camp not yet known.

Should any other information be received concerning him, such information will be at once communicated to you.

Instructions as to the method of communicating with Prisoners of War can be obtained at any Post Office.

I am,

Sir or Madam,

Your obedient Servant,

[signature]

Officer in charge of Records.

IMPORTANT.—Any change of your address should be immediately notified to this Office. It should also be notified, if you receive information from the soldier above, that his address has been changed.

Vt.30241/1250 500M. 8/39. KJL/8818 Gp.698/3 Forms/B.104—83A/6

Fig 12: Letter from the war Office to Nora notifying her of John's status as a Prisoner of War.

Roll calls took place early every morning and evening, when a bugle would call us out to stand in the same groups as our bunk aisles. The counting would rarely end with the correct numbers and it was not unusual for us to stand two or three hours, whatever the weather, until the notoriously bad counters came up with the correct numbers. Bad enough in the autumn, this became a real hazard standing in the winter snow.

Several men overbalanced at the toilets and fell into the filth - needing to be hosed down. It was bound to happen in our weakened condition. After three or four weeks a toilet block was completed. This had cut outs to squat over above just a trough in the floor. Still, this was a big improvement on the cesspits!

One day volunteers were called for with building experience - to help in further building construction. This came with the incentive of double bread ration. Thinking I would be bricklaying, I decided to give it a go but packed in after two days of carrying heavy beams and other labouring jobs.

With the camp perimeter being one mile, most of us spent a large part of the day ambling round it, under the watchful eyes of several guard towers. No other buildings were visible from the camp area, only wooded hillsides. Some men just couldn't be bothered, lying on their bunks most of the day. Soon an outbreak of stealing other people's food broke out but this was soon quashed. Anyone caught, of which there were several, had to walk round with a large placard on their back, saying, 'I am a thief.' I'm ashamed to say one man was from our own D Company.

The main topic of any conversation was always food or the lack of it. Eventually many were struck down with jaundice - which I managed to avoid. After a brief medical inspection by an Italian doctor, I was just one of many diagnosed as suffering with malnutrition but we never received any extra food. Probably just the Italians trying to show a caring attitude. Naturally everyone was gradually losing weight.

One bright spot as the colder weather set in was the arrival of our army greatcoats from the Red Cross. Without these many would not have survived. This happened after a Swiss delegation of the Red Cross had visited the camp. Shortly after their visit, we were also given Italian army jackets and trousers, with a big square red patch sewn on the back and knee. We were given a small amount of Italian lira each week to spend in a so called 'canteen', supplying toiletry items like razor blades, and Italian lather-less soap.

In October, we were given a special postcard to send home, with only specific sentences permissible like: 'I am well, hope everyone at home well.' Later we were allowed a small one-page letter, allowing us to request items of clothing and food to be sent by what came to be known as P.P.'s (personal parcels). I only ever received one out of a number sent by Nora, so there must have been wholesale pilfering in transit. She had no word from me until late November, mail taking at least a month either way. She also received a War Office letter, posting me missing, and a further one saying 'Prisoner-of-war, camp not known'. So in total, there was a six-month period when she had no idea what happened to me.

An Italian photographer was allowed in one day to take photos of small groups - I still possess mine. By coincidence, quite recently, a group photo was published in the Yorkshire Evening Post, sent in by a Leeds man who I hadn't known, but I did recognise several others.

Fig 13: Photo taken in winter 1942 at Camp Monturano POW camp by an
Italian photographer.
Back row (left to right): Roger Boyd, Harold... and an unknown soldier.
Front row: Laurie Addison, John and Jack Lovell.

In November a new building was allocated for possible
entertainment. There was no seating but we were used to
squatting! The camp was expanding all the time with new
buildings, eventually making four separate compounds. Plenty
of talent, professional and amateur, led to good concerts. My
friend, Freddie Hindle, had been in amateur dramatics at home in
Oswaldtwistle (near Accrington) and was a natural compere. The
Italians provided instruments for a small dance-band (these were
donated by civilians). Our brilliant battalion pianist, Al Hughes,
became band leader. He even composed a love song, 'This is my
night to dream'. I suppose too sentimental by today's standards,
but very popular in the camp.

Back home the Yorkshire Evening News readers had formed a Prisoner of War Club, a Wakefield branch met at the former Great Bull Hotel in Westgate. Before Christmas I received a very welcome parcel of cigarettes from the club. As I have never smoked I was able to swap them for bread - from men who would rather smoke than eat.

News started to dribble through of progress in the Desert War from the steady influx of prisoners but this was usually months old. By the year's end we knew of the American landings in Tunisia and the British loading into Algeria, so a spirit of optimism pervaded the camp, although really nothing to cheer about with the interminable roll calls, permanently cold buildings and constantly interrupted sleep. This was largely caused by the banging of the huge doors - caused by a steady stream of men heading for the toilets.

In spite of all our woes we were treated to a Christmas pantomime by Freddie and company. I think it was 'Little Red Riding Hood' with some performing in drag, courtesy of the Italians scrounging old clothing in the village. The only thing I remember about Christmas Day was spending a large part of it in the toilets with an upset stomach. With snow now lying it was impossible to keep properly warm, the only time we undressed was to deal with the ever present lice. This was only made worse by their presence in the straw palliases (sacks) on which we slept. Not always being able to brew our tea, we often had to rely on the acorn coffee for a warm drink.

I don't remember much about January and February '43, except I was cheered by letters from home. Although Nora wrote frequently, many letters were not getting through. The war news was still of a steady progress and we even dared to think there might by landings in Southern Italy, with liberation prospects. This didn't happen until several months later, bringing disastrous results for the camp, of which I will write later.

The weeks dragged on into spring, bringing warmer, sunny days, and appreciation of the fresh mountain air. Soon we were allowed to walk in small heavily-escorted groups into the village. Some of us were also allowed into the church for a short while. This was a nice gesture from the Camp Commandant.

In May we quickly received the glad news of victory for the Allies in North Africa and knew the tide had really turned. Early in June the Italians were asking for small groups to go out working, with the promise of better food and living conditions with no information about the kind of work involved. Most men declined, fearful it might mean war work in factories. For better or worse I decided to take the risk and joined a small 20-man group, with no idea where we would be going or what work awaited us.

After only a few days I was saying goodbye to my D Company mates, except for Jimmy Redmond, who had been the 7th Battalion boot repairer. Freddie and 'co' decided to stay put. Our group leader was to be Corporal Albert Machin, already in his forties and looked up to by all of us - almost as a father figure. I knew only one other, Norman Bramham. Norman was in the Signal Corps and after the war emigrated to Rhodesia as a telephone linesman. I still possess most of the group's pre-war names and addresses – we got on so well together.

We were put on the train to St. Giorgio with all our worldly possessions - just enough to fill a small haversack. We then boarded a cattle truck which was part of a whole goods train and headed north-west. Eventually we pulled into Milan rail station, where we were given the usual Italian Army meal, bully beef and biscuits, before setting off again under the curious gaze of civilian travellers.

Fig 14: Postcard sent
by John from Monturano

The next stop was Bergamo - with the Alpine foothills plainly seen from the Lombardy plain. After a walk to the outskirts of town we entered a small group of very old buildings which had been adapted to serve as Camp 62 - a small transit camp for working groups. I never discovered their original use - possibly a small factory.

After the meal of mainly vegetable stew (more substantial than at Camp 70), a bread ration and coffee we were shown our new quarters. This turned out to be a reasonably clean building with two-tier bunks. Settling down for the first night it was soon evident that the wooden bunks were crawling with horrible red bugs which only appeared when the lights were dimmed for the night. I don't think any of us slept. It was bad enough still having to cope with the lice - this was a bit too much.

Albert Machin got an interview with the Camp Commandant early the next morning and quickly had us moved to another building already occupied by Free French Foreign Legion troops from the Bir Hacheim battle. Some were from what was then French Equatorial Africa but all were very friendly, speaking mostly French. Before the war the Foreign Legion was known to recruit from all over Europe and beyond - there was even a German in the group. There was a good communal shower room and toilet block and another canteen for spending our camp lira. I don't remember having a Red Cross parcel issue there, but we were able to buy large flat slabs of chestnut cake, which at least kept us reasonably filled.

I nearly forgot to mention - the beds were bug free! There were no more roll calls either. The Italians' attitude towards us was now noticeably more friendly and relaxed. They must have realised they were not going to win the war. During our stay there, several groups like ours departed, presumably to work in agriculture. We still couldn't find out what we would be doing.

Around the end of June we were transported by lorry in a northerly direction to the Alpine foothills, to a village at the southern entrance to the Trompia valley. This was Gardone Val Trompia. Here, much to our surprise, was a new long bungalow-type building which was to be our new home. It contained new two-tier, 'bug-less' bunks, a small cooking area at one end, proper toilets and amazingly, hot water showers. There were also barred windows and a two-man 24-hour guard. Food was still a meatless stew, but this was now quite thick and with generous lumps of cheese added. The bread ration was 500 grams - a small loaf - and a piece of cheese each day. We also again got Red Cross parcels every other week. Mail was being re-directed from Camp 70 but we received no further personal parcels.

SMILING THROUGH WARTIME ORDEAL

By JOHN THORPE

THESE soldiers don't look unduly worried, but when they'd finished posing the only place they could go was to their make-shift bed...the earth of Italy.

For they were prisoners of war, and mostly came from Leeds.

This photograph was provided by one of their number, Mr Clarence Thackray, of The Laurels, Gledhow, Leeds, who is the last chap on the right in the back row.

He tells me: "I think most of the men seen were captured in the Western Desert in June, 1942, when Rommel made his big push towards Cairo.

"We are seen here in the summer of 1943 at PoW camp 70 in Montunaro, Italy, and most were from Leeds."

But how did they come to be pictured?...It was an enterprising Italian photographer who saw a chance at making some lire.

Clarence, a retired manufacturers' agent, can't remember who organised the snap, or how much it cost, but says:

"We were given a few camp lire but there was very little to spend it on, so some enterprising Italian photographer saw a way of taking it off us."

Time has erased some of Clarence's memory and he knows the soldier standing next to him but can't remember his name.

But he discovered while locked up that the other chap's father, like his own, worked at Fairburn Lawson in Leeds.

Clarence, a member of the King's Own Royal Regiment of Lancaster says that after being held prisoner in North Africa, they were shipped from Tripoli to Naples in the hold of a freighter.

Just before Italy surrendered they were locked into a train for the five-day journey to Germy, via Austria, with no food.

He ended up at a camp at Freital, about eight miles from Dresden.

Fig 15: Yorkshire Evening Post clipping about Montunaro POWs

So far so good, in every way this was a vast improvement - and now to work! On Monday morning we were taken on a short walk from the bungalow - but not into the village. We came to a dried-up river bed and our job was to start cleaning all sorts of debris and many quite large stones. These had to be manhandled on to wooden stretchers, and dumped on the bank to be carted away by civilian lorry. This proved to be quite hard work in the very hot sun but we weren't harassed in any way by the guards.

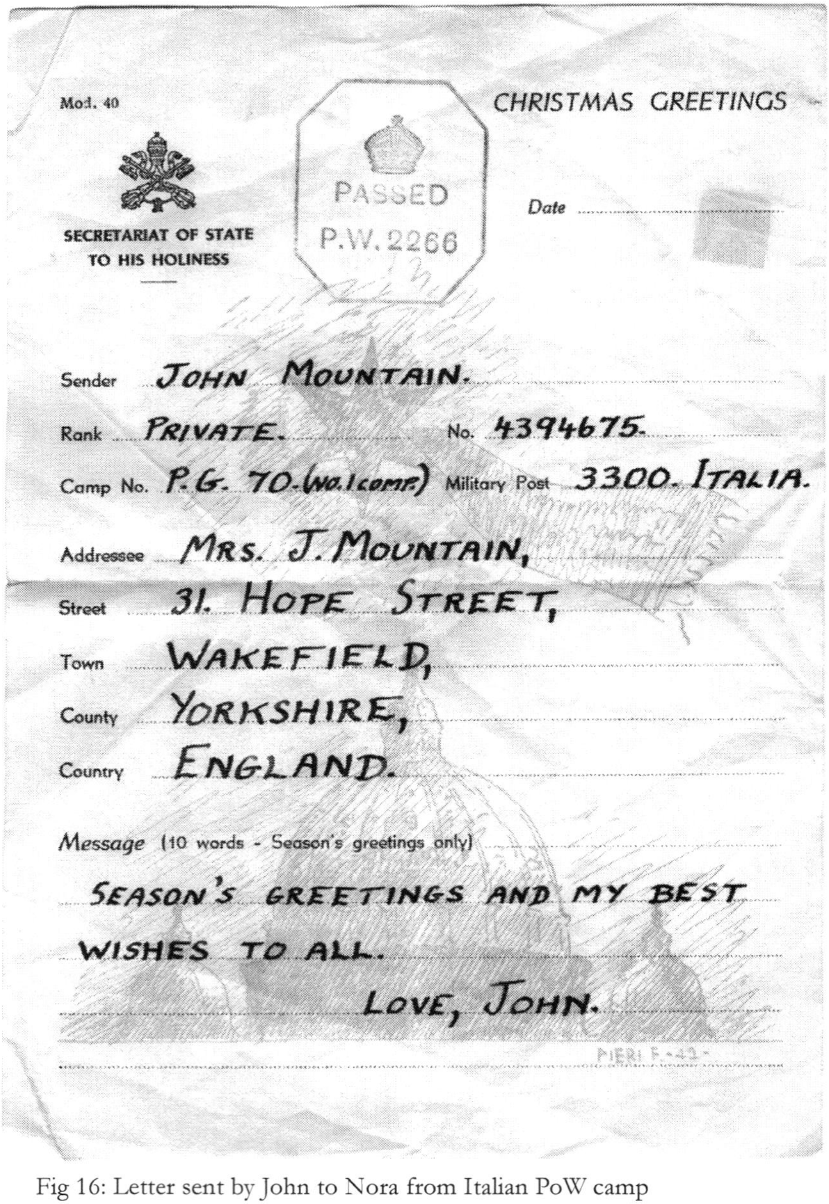

Mod. 40

CHRISTMAS GREETINGS

PASSED
P.W. 2266

Date

SECRETARIAT OF STATE
TO HIS HOLINESS

Sender __JOHN MOUNTAIN.__

Rank __PRIVATE.__   No. __4394675.__

Camp No. __P.G. 70.(No.1comp.)__ Military Post __3300. ITALIA.__

Addressee __MRS. J. MOUNTAIN,__

Street __31. HOPE STREET,__

Town __WAKEFIELD,__

County __YORKSHIRE,__

Country __ENGLAND.__

Message (10 words - Season's greetings only)

__SEASON'S GREETINGS AND MY BEST
WISHES TO ALL.
LOVE, JOHN.__

Fig 16: Letter sent by John to Nora from Italian PoW camp

Quite near to our bungalow was a small factory making the wooden butts for Beretta Machine Guns but we were never asked to work there and I didn't think what we were doing could have been classed as war work.

Early July came and we soon got news from the guards of the Allied landings on the south coast of Sicily. This, of course, gave us more thoughts of early release. My own unit, 7th Green Howards, had been fully re-enforced back in the Delta and re-joined the 8th Army in Algeria. Replacing Colonel McDonnell was with the very young Colonel 'Bunny' Seagrim who earned a posthumous Victoria Cross in the assault on the Mareth Line. The battalion was in action in the hard slog all the way up Sicily's east coast. Among the many casualties was Captain Hedley Verity. He was taken while wounded and died in captivity.

The island was finally won on 27th July. So, throughout July and early August we carried on clearing the river bed, working further up and down stream. We all of us felt the benefit of the marvellous weather, the activity and more food. Our thoughts on early release were too optimistic, with the Allied forces still being several hundred miles away. That said, they quickly made headway after crossing the Straits of Messina, the Americans advancing up Italy's west side, and 8th Army up the east.

Around the middle of August, the Italians decided to build a footbridge over the river, the first job being to drive wooden piles into the bed. What I can only describe as a Heath-Robinson contraption was erected on the river-bank, probably first used by their Roman ancestors. I find it a bit difficult to describe its construction, but I remember a large pulley wheel, mounted on top of a stout 10-foot high pole which was secured at its base. A long thick rope passing through the pulley, with a huge block of wood, possibly oak, fastened to the rope's end. When this was allowed to drop, the piles would be driven in - very fine in theory, as I was soon to discover!

Our job was to stretch out in line, like a tug-of-war team, haul on the rope to get the wood block up near the pulley, then on the command 'let go' and stand clear. I was the only one not to let go quickly enough and sailed several feet up into the air. I landed heavily (and agonisingly) on my right shoulder. If this sounds like a fictional tale, I assure you it really happened.

Two of my mates and a guard took me back to lie on my bunk, with no offer of medical help from the Italians. When the others returned after work and had their meal, I received help from an unexpected source. 'Phil' Philips, although a joiner from Notting Hill in London, had helped in a youth club, teaching boxing and knew some physiotherapy treatment. From the cook house he got some olive oil - the only thing available for massage - and got to work on my shoulder. This was so stiff I could barely raise my arm. Phil's actions gave me some relief and he promised to keep working on it in the evenings.

The next day the Italian officer, who was in charge of all the working groups in the area, came in and said I could stay off work the rest of the week, including Saturday (also a working day). However, if I couldn't turn out on Monday, I would be returned to Camp 62, Bergamo, or even to 70 - Monturano! Phil kept his word and, although still very stiff, I turned out with the others on Monday. I have always remembered his help with gratitude.

Luckily, I was given another job, bringing to an end my pile driving career! I have often wondered why they didn't just dig deep holes in the river bed, pop in the piles and encase them in concrete. We never did find out if the bridge was completed, because of changing events.

Anyway; two of us were taken to a small builder's yard in the village - our task being to make small concrete building blocks.

This was done by filling several metal presses with a mixture of fine-grained semi-dry concrete, tamping it down to make it solid and leaving it to dry in the hot sun. The next day we would turn out the blocks and start again. This proved to be an easy job as we only had a limited number of moulds - we were able to spend a large part of the day lounging in the sun. Needing to mix the small amounts of concrete had the advantage of getting my shoulder moving properly again. Stripped to the waist, the sun must have also helped, but it was really Phil who enabled me to stay with the group.

Chapter 5

As July ended, the news got better every day, with the landings in Calabria. Then, on the 8th September the Italians asked for an Armistice and unconditionally surrendered all their forces to the Allies. This led us to believe we would quickly be transported south to join our forces. Once again we should have known better.

The Germans still controlled the country and there was a quick and violent reaction to what was considered a betrayal by their former allies. General Montgomery was in charge of the British landing and sent out an order to all the main camps to stand fast, not try to escape, and await liberation. Thousands ignored the order, roaming all over the country and most were quickly recaptured and sent on their way through the Brenner Pass into Austria and Germany. A small number did manage to reach the Allied lines - some helped by civilians who almost overnight had become our friends.

Obviously the Germans weren't going to allow many thousands of prisoners to slip through their fingers to rejoin the fight. They were quick to take control, soon getting most northbound on trains, often for four or five days without food, to established camps in Germany and Austria. Some of these were killed on the way due to allied bombing or by jumping off moving trains.

Knowing nothing at all about these events, we had settled down for the night of the 8th. In the early hours we were roused and told we must get away as the Germans had already pounced on some of the other groups. Our captors were now anxious to help us on our way. The guards, like the bulk of the army, were simply throwing away their weapons, getting into civilian clothes and trying to get home. Many were caught and taken north – often receiving brutal treatment on the way from their former allies.

It was a big surprise when several villagers arrived with old clothing they had collected. That caused a scramble to get something which fitted. We were all sorry to leave our great coats but we had no choice and the villagers were happy to take them in exchange. I managed to get some decent black trousers, a blouson-type brown-checked jacket, a long black mantello (cloak) and a filthy old soft hat. So, after later acquiring a stout stick, I must have looked like a typical poor peasant!

By the time everyone was ready it was around 3.00am. After saying goodbye to the villagers we set out from the bungalow, which backed on to a very steep hillside. This was part of a chain of small peaks, which eventually lead to the High Alps.

No time could be lost getting as far away as possible before dawn but it was very hard going. One of the group was Gerald Schuster and he had more to fear than us of being recaptured, being a South African Jew. It was a complete mystery why he had survived so long - maybe because the Italians, unlike the Germans, don't seemed to have the fanatical hatred of Jewish people.

The locals had advised us to keep climbing straight up – saying we would reach a very old building. This was a mountain refuge for weary travellers of years gone by, called Refugio Maniva. As we climbed the air got much colder. When the building came into view, it proved to be made of very old stonework, only part of the four walls still stood and there was no roof at all. This was around 4.00am, with still a couple of hours to go before dawn, so we just huddled together inside.

With daylight coming it became obvious that we couldn't carry on as a group, so we split into twos and threes. I started out with Fred Penhallurick. He was several years older than me but later events proved him to be one of the best companions. Fred had been with the Northumberland Fusiliers during the Tobruk siege and was taken prisoner when it fell. He came from Cramlington - a small Northumbrian pit village and had worked in one of the coastal pits with workings going out under the sea. So he was no stranger to a tough life and hard work.

So began our first day of precarious freedom after 14-months of captivity. This should have been a reason for celebration but created a great deal more apprehension. If the Germans had arrived in Gardone they could soon by scouring the hillsides with their dogs. Without food or water we could only hope for help from any habitation we might encounter. More advice we had been given was to get out of the Trompia valley by walking over the high ground into Val Camonica. This was more populated, with a better chance of help - perhaps even the chance to get shelter until the allied armies arrived.

The last news we had was of good progress, the 8th Army having captured the Foggia airfields and continuing the advance up the east coast. The Americans were heading up the west heading for Naples and beyond.

Fred and I plodded on following a path which led into a thickly wooded area. We soon lost sight of the others and the path became harder to follow. As the day became warmer we could have done with a drink. We soon found plenty of ripe wild blackberries, which helped to alleviate the thirst. With no sign of any habitation or people we began to feel tired in the afternoon and took longer and more frequent rests. We had presumed the peak we had been climbing would lead us into Val Camonica but this eventually proved to be wrong.

As dusk was approaching we struck a better narrower path. We must have been very high as, on breaking clear of the woods, we hit the snow line, which we never expected in September. The path was veering left, making the climb not quite as steep, but still headed for the summit. As it became almost dark there was no discernible track to follow, just an icy, straight up and down slope. Now we were really in trouble. Our sticks broke trying to penetrate the frozen snow and we knew it would then be impossible to get over the top.

Luckily, as we looked down to our left, we saw a twinkling dim light, possibly about four or five hundred yards down and knew we had to get down there. The slope being far too steep and slippery to walk down, we simply got on our backsides and slid down, finishing eventually in a small farmyard - the light coming from the cottage. As there were no barking dogs to announce our arrival or any other sigh of life, we approached an open barn, containing three or four cows, obviously brought in for the night. Being totally exhausted we simply flopped down on some straw, the cows giving off some welcome warmth, and knew no more until daylight.

Here, after studying a present day map of the area, I must backtrack a little. The river-bed on which we had worked was the River Collio, with its source about ten miles to the north of Gardone. The peak Fred and I had tried to climb was Monte Seridondo and the one thing we had to do was steer clear of all roads, no doubt carrying German transport.

When the farmer appeared to get the cows out he didn't seem surprised to see us. We were able to explain, using the little Italian learned in the camps, that we were escaping English prisoners. *"Sono prisioneri Inglesi, Scapato, prego un po di mangare e acqua"* (a little food and water, please.) There didn't seem to be anyone else at the cottage.

Later we encountered other farms which were smaller than smallholdings and worked by lone elderly men. Some had emigrated after the First World War to seek a better life in America. Speaking only broken English and with the second war imminent, they had returned home to spend their remaining years. These were proving to be very harsh under German domination. Obviously regretting leaving America but, being compassionate people, they were willing to help a little.

The farmer told us several others had passed through before us the previous day, so they were either from our group or some other. Anyway, he brought out a little polenta - a maize flour mixture, made into a kind of pudding - and some red wine, for which we were truly thankful. He said we must be quickly on our way, fearful of the Germans catching him helping us. Our thoughts for our survival were still to try to find somewhere reasonably safe, to be able to get enough food, and hoping the Germans would soon be in full retreat to defend their own borders.

I have managed, with the help of the present day map and a book on tourism in the area, to follow our wanderings during the next couple of weeks. The whole area north to the high Alpine peaks, is mostly woodland with several smaller peaks. North of Seridondo, to name a few are - Monte Maniva, Monte Visigno, Monte Ario, Monte Inferni and Monte Palo. Roaming wild boar are mentioned in the book and the whole area up to the high Alps is designated National Park. There is the small Lake Idro, just two or three miles east of our route and Garda about 20 miles eastward. We, of course, knew nothing of the local geography.

Wisely we tried to avoid any more climbing and it was possible to do fairly level walking, with the advantage of finding several more small farms. If we weren't offered food there was always wine or water. Even now, there are only two main roads bordering the area, both running parallel in a north-easterly direction about 12-miles apart.

There were still plenty of wild berries in the woods and in the first afternoon we approached another very old farm cottage across an open stretch of land. The door was open - from which there was a lovely aroma of food being cooked. Uninvited, we walked in and found a bearded old man seated by a huge open fireplace. A massive iron cooking pot was suspended over the fire, in this was part of a sheep's carcass and vegetables. He was making a stew and, when we had explained who we were, he invited us to eat with him. We still possessed our small haversacks from the camp, containing tin mugs and basins, besides a few toilet items and were able to eat our fill, thanks to another very kind person.

The next couple of weeks are again a bit vague in my memory. I remember desperate days without any food - only the blackberries and water from the small streams running through the woods. I'm sure we must have thought of trying to find a main road and surrendering to the first Germans we saw. If we had been given proper shelter on any night in this short period, I feel sure it would stand out in my memory. So we must have slept rough in the woods, with nights becoming colder even though days were still warm and sunny on the lower ground. If we had tried to climb any more peaks, I surely would remember.

On a lighter note, if it could be so called, we had a small incident at this time. While crossing a small area of grassland, Fred needed urgently to relieve himself and expertly squatted down. Almost immediately he shot upright in pain from insect stings. I thought they were wasps but he insisted on them being hornets. With nothing to alleviate the agony of several stings, he must have suffered for at least a day or two.

From here my memory is crystal clear. Approaching yet another peak we suddenly spotted what appeared to be a small and very old village clinging almost at the top of the slope. Down to our left, about half a mile away, there was the end of a road, possibly only one vehicle wide. This served the village but the ground was too steep for it to extend all the way. Tired and weak through lack of sleep and food we had no choice but to ask for help - even if Germans were present.

The first cottage to come into view was at the top of a rough path leading from the road end. The present day map shows a minor road to the village, so now being in the tourist area, the cottages may still be there as holiday homes. A middle-aged lady opened the door, at first seeming shocked by our appearance, but accepted the fact we were English recently escaped prisoners.

Being very sympathetic, we were soon getting water and polenta. Then she led us to a barn at the cottage side where she revealed, much to our amazement, Phil Phillips (who got my arm moving at the camp) and Bill Blagburn (a Geordie also from our group) - lying there in the straw.

The village was Presegno di Lavenone - a few miles from the small town of Lavenone, which we must have missed in our wanderings. In a direct line on the map, Presegno lies about 12-miles to the north-east of Gardone but we had probably covered twice that distance when avoiding climbing peaks. The lady was Signora Maria Campagnoli, a deeply religious Roman Catholic, as were all the villagers.

There were only about two dozen cottages, but there was a lovely tiny church, which everyone attended. Maria's husband soon arrived from their smallholding, which was hidden from our view over the other side of the hill, with another very lame middle-aged man who was also deaf and dumb, and only ever addressed as Il Muto. We were accepted without question after Maria had spoken - obviously with much sympathy for us - *gli povere Inglesi*. I'm sure most of them contributed to our food supply with unbelievable generosity - considering everything had to be carried the half-mile climb from the road end.

We all had shared hopes that the Germans would soon be driven from their country but also a real fear that the enemy would catch them sheltering us. They stressed it was up to us to watch the valley road for any sight of transport approaching. In the meantime, we offered to help in any of their activities, Fred and I doing work on the smallholding and rebuilding a dry-stone wall leading to the cottage. The other two helped in the village and were offered another place to sleep, leaving the barn for us.

The village priest and his sister also got involved in our welfare. Each evening they welcomed us into their small apartment in the church building to play a card game and drink acorn coffee. A few other people would also arrive and there was much fun sitting at a large table, passing the cards around and chanting a verse. The game was called 'Frig-a-Tag' but that's all I remember about it, I'm afraid. The most memorable thing in my memory was their possession of a well concealed small radio and only brought out in the evening to hear the news from London. Now that things elsewhere were going well it was an amazing lift to our morale.

There were days when the people would get understandably nervous, perhaps when someone had been to Lavenone and heard rumours of German atrocities. We would walk through the village early morning and disappear for the day into the dense woodland, taking a little food and water. With hindsight, we needn't have worried, no enemy was ever seen. Perhaps they were now thin on the ground, with many being sent to the battlefront. One evening on the radio we heard that the Germans had put a price on our heads. The magnificent sum of £20 to anyone giving information leading to the re-capture of an escaping prisoner.

One day, while out at our job, a middle-aged man approached us, seemingly from nowhere. He certainly hadn't climbed the hill and was quite decently dressed and cliaming to be an escaping Yugoslav army officer, a member of a partisan group actively harassing the enemy nearer his homeland to the east. He was looking for recruits to join the band, and saying he had already recruited several Brits. He spoke good English and offered to supply us with weapons and decent food. He had possibly got some of our working group, as we had not yet seen any of the others. As we were already making other plans so we declined.

In October the news from the south was not so good after Naples falling in the west and the Salerno landings, the 8th Army losing 50th Division (who returned home to prepare for invading the continent) the winter rains in the Appenines halted the advance. We started to think we might be overstaying our welcome and, although nothing was being said to that effect, we felt it was maybe time to move on.

Before I proceed further, I must again apologise for backtracking a little. From our first days in Presegno, having already mentioned the existing devout Catholicism in the village, Maria tried hard to convert Fred and me – without success, of course. However we could hardly refuse to kneel on the bare earth cottage floor each evening, and say prayers led by her. This included teaching us the Ave Maria and Lord's Prayer in Latin and in the very similar Italian. We also went to the Sunday morning church service. The first time we could hardly believe our eyes when, in full view of their women-folk, the men lined up and relieved themselves on the side wall. Anyway, enough about that!

By the middle of November, we were still trying to decide whether to set out when another lone escaper arrived, dressed like us in rough civilian clothes but with a shock of blond, curly hair spilling out of his dirty cap. His appearance was nowhere near the Italian peasant look! In fact had he been dressed in German uniform, he would have been the image of Hitler's 'master race' of blond Aryans!

This was Corporal J.W. (Steven) Stevenson of the Sherwood Foresters, and from Silverdale, Staffordshire. His plan was to try for Switzerland with the help of an old map he had acquired on his travels so far. He was very tired and hungry and needed a week or so before setting out. He asked all four of us to join him. Fred and I were immediately enthusiastic, but the other two decided to stay on, and we never saw them again. Explaining our intentions to Maria, she managed to get help for Steve with food and he stayed with us in the barn for a few days.

The news was still not good, with the battlefront grinding to a halt - making us still more determined to try for the border. We knew from Steve's map that the nearest border point was to the north-west but that route would involve crossing too many roads. The best way was to head north or north-east for a long distance, before turning westerly. Instead of a 40-mile trek, it would be more like 60. By again referring to the present map, there are numerous peaks and valleys over the whole area, making very little level ground for walking.

With numerous good wishes and 'Arrivedercis,' we set out one cold but sunny morning on a woodland path at the back of the village, which seemed to head north. We were well supplied with polenta and chestnut cake, so no immediate food worries. I still remember having the large slab of cake stuffed inside my blouson-type jacket. A light snow had fallen overnight on the already frost hardened ground. Luckily, with the day-long sunshine, we could keep roughly northerly, but we probably only managed about five or six miles on the first day, finding suitable paths through the wooded hillsides. I don't remember seeing any signs of habitation on that first walk, so we must have slept rough in the quite thick undergrowth, or more likely stamping about to keep warm most of that cold night.

Looking again at my map, the area up to the high Alps is showing several smaller peaks. Mounts Maniva, Matto, San Gallo, Mattoni, Frerone and Frisozzo to name a few, with areas of woodland and grassland in the valleys. Being still in Vale Trompia with the main road between Brescia and Edolo and beyond running north-east and the border to the west we determined this was the road we would have had to cross to get into Val Camonica. We were told in Gardone we would be more likely to get help here but decided the road was much too dangerous to attempt.

Not long into the second day's walk with our spirits revived by a warm sun, I remember very clearly striding out on a fairly level path, still in woodland. I rounded a right-hand bend into more open ground and ran straight into about 20 German soldiers! They were resting either side of the path, smoking, obviously having a break from an exercise routine. Steve whispered, "Keep walking, don't look back" and, unbelievably, we sailed straight through the whole bunch without any challenge from them. I think I said *buon giorno* about six times and received similar greetings in answer. We must have really looked the part of scruffy country yokels - but why not one of them spotted Steve's golden curls we could never understand - especially as they must have been warned to look out for escapers. Maria's prayers for a safe journey were truly answered that day!

On we went, without challenge and, as the saying goes, 'things can only get better' - and indeed they did. After having got well clear of 'Hitler's finest', we neither saw nor heard any sign of pursuit. So we stopped for a breather and self congratulation. Then, breaking clear of the woods into a valley of grassland still trying to head north-east (based on the sun's position), we came to a small isolated farm, with a dirt road leading westward. Presumably this connected with the main Brescia – Breno - Edolo road.

The occupants were yet more of the returned English-speaking US emigrants. After saying we were English escapees trying to reach Switzerland we were made welcome. They gave us food and wine and we were sent merrily on our way. I say merrily, because the wine must have gone to our heads and I remember ambling along the valley in a semi-drunken state - singing as if without a care in the world!

My memory of the next few days becomes a bit vague but we must have made reasonable progress, possibly seven or eight miles per day, because of the eventual outcome. We must also have found food and shelter for the cold nights, otherwise we would have found it difficult to survive. Since leaving Presegno, I have since calculated, we walked a minimum of 40-miles before turning west towards the border. if we allow for diversions to avoid the higher peaks, it could easily have been over 50 miles. Knowing it would be necessary to cross the Edolo road into Valcamonica at some point we had no choice but to push on and chance it.

On the sixth day of the walk and, after following another woodland path, we suddenly burst into open ground stood on a high bank, looking down on the Edolo road. Having looked to left and right, we established there was no sighting of any traffic. To the right, however, stood a German soldier about 200 yards away on the far side of the road. He was obviously on sentry duty - guarding whatever was in the trees behind. Whatever this was we couldn't tell as it wasn't in our view. Could this have been a camp in the woods for the German unit which we had brazenly walked through earlier? It seems highly probable.

Without hesitation, we had a mad scramble down the bank and were over the road and into the woods on the far side - praying we hadn't been seen.

About an hour beyond this we were hurrying on and still on high ground but struggling to make progress due to the snow-covering. The light was fading and we saw, possibly a half-mile away down to our left, a few glimmers of light which could have been Edolo. The priority now as ever, was to find food and shelter for the night and, amazingly, in the trees just clear of the path stood a large old shack - maybe a woodcutter's dwelling previously.

A young man came to the door, not seeming surprised to see us and with our usual introduction, 'Prisioneri Inglese, scapato', we were allowed to enter. There were several other young men who told us they were part of a resistance group, partisans and lately of the Italian army operating in the area to harass the Germans, when and by whatever means possible. They were just one of many groups active throughout the whole country north of the River Po. Some had managed to keep their rifles and other small calibre weapons but were also being supplied larger weapons, ammunition and food by allied air drops - the planes operating from the southern Foggia airfields.

The group seemed to have an abundance of food and wine and, after giving us plenty to eat and drink, offered to escort us to the nearest border-crossing point. This was on the outskirts of the Swiss village of Campocologno at the tip of a small part of Swiss territory protruding into Italy. On the map this looks like a small thumb. We were told they had already got others safely over, giving us real hope that our goal was in sight. They asked for our army identity, name, rank and number, in order to confirm to Allied forces, when they finally reached the north that they had seen us safely over.

Another 16 months were to go by before our forces broke through into Austria, signalling the end of German forces in Italy. At this time (December '43), the advance was mostly at a standstill because of the terrible weather in the Appenines. In hindsight, we made the right decision earlier not to linger.

We were told the safest time to start out would be around midnight, with three of them taking each one of us but spaced well out in twos, about 100 yards apart. Fortified against the cold snowy night by another (small) drink of wine and with chestnut cake to carry in case of hold ups, we were on our way. In spite of the snow the path through the trees was easily followed but by no means level going, meandering left and right, up and down.

On my map, there is marked 'Passo di Guspessa', which must have been the route through the hills we were taking. After about two or three hours, I could distinguish pin-points of light, way down the slopes to our left and could hear dogs barking. My guide said this was the town of Tirano, situated on a minor road which at some point we must have crossed but I don't recall doing so. By now, we must have really felt the strain with no break, just steadily plodding on, when at first light on 6th December I remember spotting two red and white posts, only just visible in the bushes and knew we had made it.

After we gave the guides our thanks and good wishes they turned back and were soon out of sight, no doubt three, very tired men by the time they got back to the hut. Without their help we probably wouldn't have succeeded - I have never forgotten them, nor all those good people who helped us to survive.

So, with one stride, we had finally reached safety.

Chapter 6

The first building we saw was large and wooden just a short distance away, which we later discovered was a disused school. Setting off down the steep snowy slope we had only covered a few yards when, from our right, several skiers bore down on us, giving us a real fright. They were wearing what we thought were German grey field uniforms but we were soon put at our ease by their leader stating in perfect English they were a Swiss army border patrol, who wear the same colour uniforms as the Germans. Obviously used to dealing with escapers, we were taken into the school and found several people - men, women and children - lying sleeping on the floor. We later discovered these were Italian Jews from Tirano, who had struggled through the night over the top to safety, leaving their homes in fear of an imminent German round-up.

Soon some Swiss Red Cross ladies appeared - giving each of us a large jug of steaming hot milky cocoa and some bread and cheese. Talk about manna from heaven! We were then allowed to sleep on the floor until about midday when, under army escort, we were put on a small train and taken 24-miles along the Upper Engadine valley to the small town of Samedan, which is just two miles east of St. Moritz, the well known ski resort.

On arrival, we were taken to the local swimming baths and stripped of all our filthy clothing, which was taken to be burnt. We had wonderful hot showers, put into what I can only describe as a de-lousing chamber and sprayed with a disinfectant powder. Next we went to another room to see large piles of good second-hand clothing, obviously donated. We were allowed to take our pick to become fully clothed. I got a good quality tweed double-breasted jacket in grey herring-bone, with trousers to match, pullover, shirt and underwear. I got dressed and we felt like civilized human beings again. We were then taken to yet another room where, to our surprise, sitting at a desk in full uniform were two British army officers. They introduced themselves as MI9 agents - a military intelligence organisation set up by Churchill early in the war to seek information about the enemy from prison camps and escapers.

Here I must mention that, by late 1944, there were 5,000 ex-prisoners in Switzerland. These were British and British Empire citizens - not just from Italian camps but from all over Europe. Some were even from France who had disappeared into the countryside after Dunkirk - perhaps working on farms. Others were RAF men who, having been shot down, managed to evade capture. A total of 28 damaged American Fortress and Liberator bombers managed to land in the flatter northern part of Switzerland. It was obvious that, although remaining neutral, the Swiss were very much on our side. However, always aware that if the Germans decided to invade it would be impossible with their tiny army to defend the northern half which was easily accessible to German armour. The Swiss had, over several years, constructed a defence system right across the Alps, known as the Reduit (redoubt). We later learned that with our Government's permission, we could be armed and help in their defence. Thankfully, this never happened, Hitler having a bigger worry on his hands - the Allied invasion of France.

I don't remember how long our interrogation lasted but they wanted a comprehensive run-down on all our activities since being taken prisoner. In addition to personal details, rank, name, number and home address for War Office information. Then we told them all about the good people of Gardone, Presegno, the Italian guides on our final walk - all of which was noted down. They told us the help we received would be acknowledged at the war's end. Next they wanted to know the route we had taken and if we had seen any buildings which might be producing war material? The only thing in our memory which might have been useful, was seeing the German sentry on the Brescia-Edolo road, obviously guarding something out of our sight in the woods. By the time they had finished with us it was too late in the day to move us on, so we were taken somewhere else locally, for food and bed for the night.

Here I feel I must divert a little to mention my dear wife, Nora. Of her endurance in most difficult conditions - walking to and from work, being alone in winter, the blacked-out streets and doing an unpleasant job. There were two separate periods of several months in both 1942 and '43 when she had no idea what was happening to me. In 1942 she only received a War Office telegram saying 'Missing, believed prisoner' and later, from the Red Cross, 'Prisoner, camp not known'. After my last letter, sent from Gardone and delivered in September '43 she didn't hear anything until she received a War Office telegram on 29th December. This was sent via Infantry records in York and notified Nora that I had escaped and reached Switzerland.

Carrying on with our journey; it was back to Samedan station, where we were put on a train - still under escort. We joined around a dozen other escapers including two South Africans and an Australian. We headed north for about 70 miles - at first close to the border with Austria, then tiny Lichtenstein and ending at Rorschach at the eastern end of Lake Constance (or as it's known locally, Bodensee) with the German shoreline clearly visible. We then transferred to a small mountain railway. After an ascent of about four miles we came to the snowbound village of Heiden, in Canton Appenzell. In the same way Britain is divided into counties, Switzerland has cantons. Most of the north of the country is German speaking - about 70 percent of the population. 25 percent speak French and most of the remaining 5 percent Italian. There is also a dialect, commonly known as Romansch or Shwitzer Deutsh, which is very different from German.

After leaving the train we plodded through deep snow, halting at a small hotel, 'Gletzerhugel' - which was to be our home. There were no paying guests - it functioned as a café and bar during the day. A wide entrance hall in the centre seperated the café-bar at the left end of the building – we occupied the right wing. This had been the dining room, toilets and a small kitchen, where we would wash and shave in the morning. Straw palliases, army-style, were laid out on the floor with blankets. A British officer arrived to explain the situation for ex-prisoners. As there were such large numbers, they were spread over the northern half of the country in small towns or villages, and known as detachments. He, Captain Ricketts, had charge of Heiden, with a central control of all detachments at Wil, near St. Gallen, who in turn had direct contact with the War Office.

Food was supplied in special hot containers by a central cookhouse in the village. We would be kept occupied by courses in various subjects, with instructors being supplied from and interchangeable between detachments. Military-style parades were forbidden by the Swiss - which was no problem to us! We were forbidden to leave the village though this was not possible anyway with a money allowance of only a few Swiss franks a week. This was enough for a visit to the small cinema and a few living essentials. We were allowed to rent an excellent radio for only a few franks This was a real blessing for the evenings with quite deep snow lying and us previously starved of proper news for long periods. The cinema showed only German films but we could laugh at the propaganda newsreels about how, with all Hitler's secret weapons, they would still win the war. Some nights we could easily hear the RAF bombing on the north shore of Constance followed, during the day, by the Americans.

We had plenty of free time. On some afternoons we would trudge around the surrounding hills through the snow and breathing in the cold and clear mountain air. An interesting feature of Heiden was the grave of Henri Dunant buried in the village cemetery which was near to the railway station. Henri was founder of the International Red Cross, to which we owed so much. I have no doubt the whole Appenzell canton will now be a popular tourist attraction - with skiers heading for the higher Alpine slopes.

As I write, Nora just told me of an incident while she was walking home from work in the late summer of 1943. During a violent thunderstorm lightning struck her brolly, sending it flying from her grasp but thinks her rubber-soled shoes saved her from injury. She remembers Christmas that year not being a happy time for anyone with all the wartime restrictions, severe food rationing, the black-out, and still having no news of me until the telegram on the 29th. The only holidays allowed were the 25th and 26th

Fig 17 - Gossau, Switzerland with the family
Knellwold. John is scond from the left.

- which had been usual for most workers before the war. The
mail to and from Switzerland, as from Italy, took three to four
weeks, so it would be late January '44 before I received a letter,
five months after the last one to reach Italy.

My main memory of the remaining weeks of '43 was getting
our battle-dress uniform and a Royal Air Force great-coat - again
courtesy of the Red Cross. We really needed these in the bitterly

cold snowy weather and, with minimum of heat in our room, the coat served as an extra blanket. The food was basic but plentiful - a million times better than prison camp life.

Progress on the Italian front was still very slow but preparations at home for the invasion were well under way, helped by the massive American build-up. Through the remaining winter months, nothing of note stands out in my memory, except a lecture from a member of the British Embassy Staff about The William Beveridge Report – the plans for the future health service with total free health care for all. The village hall proved to be a most useful lecture room.

In the middle of March I was called to see Captain Ricketts. He told me there was a course in building construction planned for would-be post-war bricklayers. This was to be held at the lovely small town of Gossau near St. Gallen. As my trade was known he asked if I would be willing to pass on some of my knowledge? Off I went and soon settled in with what was to be a new set of friends in the Gossau detachment. We were about a hundred men, billeted in a large two-storey building in the town centre which I think had been a small factory. The floor, as in Heiden, was laid out in palliases. The man next to me was Sam Patinnson, a bricklayer from Country Durham who was a few years older than me. We soon became good friends. He had also been recruited to help with the course, which was headed by a South African major and a British captain. However, it did not start immediately due to difficulty in obtaining building materials, especially cement. We got started early in May with about a dozen enthusiastic pupils.

There were other courses taking place in the other trades, with the two officers giving indoor lectures. It was featured in a unique monthly newspaper, with news and pictures from all the detachments and the latest war news. I still possess a few copies of *Marking Time* which, in a way I suppose we were, they have yet to yellow with age. As a side note I'll point out that the cover of this book is based on one of the *Marking Time* covers. Sam and I had interesting talks with the major, as the South African method of brickwork bonding is what we call 'Dutch bond', which is very rarely used in Britain. The bonds mainly used here are Flemish, old English, garden wall and, most commonly used, stretcher.

It became a real pleasure to be usefully occupied in the warm and sunny weather. Evenings were spent walking and sitting in a lovely park. A small group of us would go to the beer garden of an inn to enjoy a glass of beer or cider but that would usually be the limit, for lack of finances.

I had one unpleasant experience in Gossau relating to dental work. My teeth must have been in a bad way because 16 fillings were done, paid for through the British Embassy. The lady dentist gave me a lot of pain, the drill frequently getting too hot and she never seemed to realise how it was hurting me. I was glad when, after a few weeks the treatment came to an end.

A few weeks into the course the major showed me a small plan of what was known in the army as an Aldershot oven. This was a small brick structure with origins in the First World War - a kind of enclosed barbecue. These were for use in a field kitchen and I was asked to go and set it up at another detachment. This was in a village of which I don't recall the name but which could have been Degersheim - also in the Wil area. When told I could take someone else to mix the mortar I chose 'Ginger' Hudson, a likeable lad from Grange-over-Sands in the Morecambe Bay area - we were to be be lodged and fed with the detachment. We went with our little bag of tools and essentials, return rail tickets and no escort – and had a very nice few days. The oven was easy to construct and, although I never did discover if it was a success, was confident it would be.

Fig 18 - John
in Switzerland -
January 1944

After this distraction we went back to Gossau, the course and
the exciting news of the D-Day landings. Much later learning
that my own unit, 7th Green Howards, 50th Division, were in
the first wave to hit 'Gold' beach on 6th June. I believe it was
in that same week we were told it might be possible to obtain
work in the civilian building industry until such time when we
would be leaving the country. We would earn a little money, with
free board and lodgings. Apparently there was a big shortage of
labour, owing to all the fit young men having to do a period of
army service.

Sam and I quickly volunteered and, on a Saturday in June, Herr Herman Stutz, a building contractor, arrived and took us in his car to Romanshorn. This was a small town 10 miles northwest of Rorschach, on the Lake Constance shoreline - almost opposite Friedrichshafen, the important German u-boat-building town. He saw us safely lodged in a small lakeside hotel. Having told us we would be picked up early on Monday morning to take us to work he gave us time to settle in over the weekend.

Early on Monday morning the site foreman called for us and took us to an ironmonger's shop to buy tools. He spoke no English but, as we had acquired some basic German, we managed to communicate well enough to get by. A problem immediately arose - the Swiss bricklaying trowel was simply a rectangular blade. Not unlike our plasterer's trowel but with the handle at one end, instead of the middle. We explained about the kite-shaped blade we were used to and, without more ado, we trotted off to a blacksmiths. On our instruction he cut the blades to our satisfaction as had been done with several trowels for the Gossau course. The remaining few tools were basically the same but for building corners there was only the plumb bob on a string, which had to be swung, and the corner bricks aligned with the string. This was difficult in a strong wind but it was what we had been used to at home. Only after the war did the metre long plumb level become available.

The small site was building semi-detached houses near the lake-side. We set to work on a pair already partly built to bedroom height. The bricks were the part hollow type and we were given a labourer but I don't remember seeing any more bricklayers on site in the time we were there. When we reached roof height we were moved to another site. I clearly remember the bombing of Friedrichshafen and the surrounding districts during our time in Romanshorn. About mid-morning the American Fortresses and

Liberators would arrive over the target from their Italian bases, giving Sam and I a grandstand view of the merciless bombing. The RAF arriving nightly to do the same - which we also saw from our hotel room, which looked out over the lake.

In July Herr Stutz arrived to move us to another site in a village a few miles south of the lake. I'm not sure of the name as, looking at the map, there is a cluster of villages in quite a small area but Herisau would be the most likely location. Again we arrived on a Saturday afternoon. We stopped in front of a neat bungalow and Herr Stutz introduced us to an elderly Austrian widow. She was to be paid for providing us with bed and breakfast and we had a lovely spotlessly clean room with twin beds. After leaving our belongings, for which we had now bought small cases, we moved on to the village butcher. They were to supply us with midday sandwiches and a main meal a short walk away when work finished on the site. The new building, which was in the early stages of construction, was to be a store for fresh fruit - mainly apples for cider making.

On the Monday morning we met our new workmates who were a few older labourers and three or four teenage bricklayers - none yet fully trained. The responsibility for the brickwork was down to us. The foreman was elderly and German-born - he proved to be really friendly towards us. The long working days were sunny and hot but with a splendid virtually un-rationed dinner every evening at the butchers we got to be on top form. Every afternoon the foreman would appear on the scaffold with a large bottle of beer each, which was really appreciated in the heat and during the long working days - 7.30am to 6.00pm and Saturday morning. We were still restricted in travelling elsewhere but had no inclination to do so anyway. Evenings were pleasantly spent in one of the village café-bars, socialising with the locals and picking up a bit more German! One evening, instead of the fairly weak bottled beer, we were persuaded to try the popular short drink, schnapps. This was colourless but very potent and we later regretted it - having a terrific hangover next morning.

One job on the store proved to be very strenuous - laying the concrete floor. This was done when we had got the brickwork half-way up. The only mechanical aid in use was a temperamental old mixer. The mixed concrete was loaded into large double-wheeled barrows and then pushed by two men up a ramp on to the floor level. This went on for several days - Sam and I volunteered to go in after the evening meal, when the concrete had dried enough, to trowel it to a smooth surface - at home this was called 'rubbing up'. It was then a relief to get back on the brickwork.

In the middle of August came the great news that an American invasion fleet had landed on the Riviera in southern France and was already advancing up the Rhone Valley towards the Swiss border at Geneva - eventually continuing to the Rhine and Germany. All this was very exhilarating news because we had been made aware of plans that, as soon as the Americans reached the border, we were to evacuate into France. So all we internees were eagerly listening to radio news every day. The Swiss must also have been relieved - knowing that the end was in sight of having to feed a small army of foreigners.

Since late January the mail from home had been fairly regular, but still took three or four weeks and my own letters home were still being censored by our own officers. The only person I met in Switzerland from my own unit was Lieutenant Millington-Buck, who had commanded 17 Platoon.

Chapter 7

The work continued until the morning of 8th October when, the building still not completed and without any previous warning, an officer arrived from Wil HQ and said, "Right lads, stop working, you're on your way home". We very gladly gave our tools to the young apprentices and, with much handshaking, said *auf-wiedersehen* to all. We then went to the butchers to thank them for all the lovely meals, then on to collect our bits and pieces from the bungalow and to thank the kind lady for looking after us so well. I forget what transported us but we were taken to Sirnach, a village just on the outskirts of Wil, and put in what seemed to be the local community centre. This was already almost full with men from the detachments. It was a case of bedding down on the floor for the night, in the belief that morning would see us on the train to Geneva as there was a direct rail link from Wil. To everyone's frustration the 9th was spent kicking our heels until, on the 10th, we were on our way. Also on the train were a few familiar faces from the Bergamo and Gardone camps as well as Lieutenant Millington-Buck - presumably to keep us in good order.

I had kept in touch with Fred Penhallurick, famous you may remember for squatting on a hornet's nest! He had left Heiden soon after me to work on a construction site at Schaffhausen, at the western end of Constance. He had been injured by the collapse of a partly built concrete wall and spent several days in hospital with an injured leg. We were glad to meet up again on the train and to be able to travel home together.

The journey would be about 300 miles and passed through Zurich. On reaching Geneva we transferred to a French train, bound for Marseilles - I don't remember any delays during the swap. This got us thinking "there'll be a boat waiting, we'll be in Britain in a couple of days" - but how wrong we were! On approaching Annecy, the train was held up. While stationary another stopped alongside, full of American troops en route to the battlefront. Through the open windows, one shouted, "What's it like up there, buddy?" obviously thinking we'd been at the front. I can't remember what his reply was, once we told him who we were, no doubt something obscene!

On we went through Chambery, Grenoble and Aix-en-Provence to Marseilles, having seen the destruction wrought by bombing and battle and, nearer the coast, shell-fire damage from before the landings. Upon arriving at the docks area it became obvious with so much destruction it would be impossible for anything but small boats to come alongside. In a short while that's exactly what happened. A motorboat came in to ferry us out to an American troopship, which was anchored about a mile offshore. This was joined by another boat but it took a few hours, with the boat's limited loading space, to get us all away. Our boat was soon bobbing about like a cork, with a heavy swell running. As we drew nearer to the ship, we could see it was a long way to deck level. We were wondering how on earth would we reach it? We would be at least 20-feet from the water line! The penny soon dropped when we pulled in close to a large scrambling net hanging from the deck. When the swell took us close in two men at a time would climb onto the net. One hand would grab the net, the other holding our case. This on its own was no mean feat but we then had to scramble up one-handed with two hefty sailors above to haul us aboard. How everyone got safely aboard must have been a minor miracle - it tested our physical condition to a limit.

It came as a revelation to see the comfortable two-tier bunks when shown our quarters. This was a complete contrast to the grotty and crowded hammock-slung decks of our own troopships. The food was excellent, with lashings of ice-cream and soft drinks. As we headed south, it was obvious we weren't going to be home in a hurry. After two pleasant days as guests of the US navy we came ashore at Salerno in southern Italy - without needing the scramble net. There had been heavy fighting here during the '43 landings. The front line was at that time much further north but still short of the River Po. Fred and I could never have held out in the Alps for a whole year.

My next memory is of a huge tented rest-camp, set up on the beautiful beach for American troops withdrawn from the front for a rest. Everything was highly organised, so much more efficient than in our own army but they seemed to have endless resources at their disposal. Our stay lasted a week, during which there were thorough medical checks. Otherwise it was just a matter of whiling away the time between meals, mostly resting on the beach in the warm autumn sunshine. The food was distributed from a large field-kitchen, at which it was necessary to queue with our tin plates and dixies, taking the food back to the tent to eat. One morning a British officer, one of several at the camp, walked bold as brass straight to the head of the long queue. He was expecting to be served first but an American sergeant who was supervising the food, brought him quickly down to terra firma saying, "Get to the back, buddy, no priorities, we're all equal here". So he had to hear all the cat-calls on the way back. We were all wearing Swiss watches, which the Americans were eager to buy, but I don't think many were sold.

On or about 24th October we were taken by American army transport to Naples where we saw the devastation caused by the bombing and invasion a year previously. There was still very little evidence of re-building or of easing the utter poverty of the poor starving population. The dock area was as badly wrecked as Marseilles. We were directed to a large upturned ship with just the bottom showing above the water line. It was necessary to walk over this to board our homeward bound troopship, HM Staffordshire. On being shown to our quarters we were surprised to see two-tier bunks - not the useless hammocks. Obviously a lesson had been learnt from our allies.

Since the African coast had been cleared of the enemy by the May '43 victory, it was no longer necessary for shipping to sail thousands of miles round the Cape, saving several weeks on the journey to and from the UK. Even so, it took our ship 11 days to reach Liverpool. One night was spent in Gibraltar harbour for re-fuelling but we got little sleep owing to a u-boat alarm and the intermittent boom of depth charges for a good part of the night. Food on board was a bit of a let-down, we must have been spoiled by the American goodies. Sailing through Biscay nearly everyone was sea-sick, myself included. This we attributed to the fatty pork we ate at lunchtime. I can still remember the thrill of being just days away from home after three and a half eventful years away.

Upon docking in Liverpool on 4th November, we were told to expect a customs' search, but this didn't happen. Instead we were waved straight on to a waiting train - arriving in Amersham,

Buckinghamshire at tea-time. After being fed there were more medical and army records checks - with the promise of being allowed to go home on the 5th. We were then given six weeks leave, ration cards and rail warrants and sent on our respective and joyful ways.

At Amersham we had been given new uniforms and other necessary items but no cumbersome equipment or arms. By tea-time on the 5th I was entering number 31 Hope Street. I was expected, Nora having received notice by telegram, which we still possess. She was wearing a lovely pale blue dress and looked not a day older. It is impossible to describe the emotion and joy of re-union - unforgettable. I think we were both speechless for the first few moments, then it all came flooding out and it was as though I had never been away and then I was welcomed home by Nora's parents.

We were back to reality the following day - with Nora having to carry on with the Air Ministry clothing store job. I met her every evening to walk her home and we had lovely evenings, just happy to be together again. The following weeks flew by as the 16th and the end of my leave drew near. We were to be parted for yet another Christmas. Out of the blue a letter arrived from York Infantry records, saying my leave would be extended to cover Christmas and New Year, along with more ration cards and a rail warrant for 2nd January '45. With instructions to report to Farnley Park, Otley, where a hutted camp was being used as a rehabilitation centre for ex-POWs.

I must now mention my best friend from school days, Len Hartley. Only a few weeks before I got home, while flying as navigator-gunner in a Mosquito fighter-bomber, he was shot down and killed over Belgium. Len had visited Nora several times while on leave. We visited his parents on my leave, grief stricken at the loss of a fine eldest son and fearing for Dougie, their younger son, who

Fig 20 - Len Hartley's grave in Belgium

was in Burma with the 14th Army. Two years later he returned safely and a memorial service for Len was held at Wrenthorpe Church, with his sister, Ruth, singing 'I know that my redeemer liveth' beautifully. I was given the honour of unveiling a small stained glass window, close to the pulpit and choir stall where we sang together as teenagers, which was donated by Mr and Mrs Hartley. I still possess a photo of his grave in Belgium, showing his parents on one of their visits.

Back to December '44 and, with my leave extension into New Year, Nora and I were invited to spend Christmas at Jim Mason's home. He lived with his wife Margaret, at her parents' large cottage in Horton-in-Ribblesdale - five miles north of Settle. Jim came home on leave from the Rhine Army, as it was then called, and we had an emotional re-union on the small station - where he had worked as booking-clerk. There had been two and a half years since we last saw each other, there was much filling in to do. He had survived all the desert battles, the invasion of Sicily and Italy and the D-Day landing on 'Gold Beach'. He had received rapid promotion from corporal to RQMS (regimental quartermaster sergeant). This had given him a better chance of survival when almost all of our 7th Battalion became casualties. This included the CO who replaced Colonel McDonnell with whom I was captured. Major D.A. (Bunny) Segrim (aged 23) was awarded a posthumous Victoria Cross at the Mareth line, Tunisia, 20th and 21st March '43, and Sergeant Major Stan Hollis, a Victoria Cross on D-Day, at Mont Fleury and Crepen, 6th June '44. Jim didn't think I would have survived through it all as a PBI (poor bloody infantryman). Almost all the old familiar names were casualties. The remnants of the battalion who got safely back to the Nile delta after the big withdrawal were all promoted to form the nucleus of a new 7th Battalion. After a period of rest and training this re-joined the 8th Army in the advance into Algiers and Tunisia.

Returning to our Christmas in Horton - we had a wonderful few days. After this we had to return - Nora went back to work and I found myself at Farnley Park, Otley. This was a Nissen-hutted camp set on a snowy hillside. I met several familiar faces, but most of the men sent from the Italian camps to Germany had not yet been released. The reason for being here was to get us back to A1 fitness. The war on the continent and in south-east Asia was not yet over and there was always a shortage of trained infantry. There were days of runs over the cold snowy countryside, with weapon training. This included the PIAT anti-tank gun, which was new to me and had a kick like a mule when fired, and the Sten gun, a very light and easy to handle weapon. There were also lectures and much PT.

There were several times I managed to get home for a few hours - even though officially we weren't allowed beyond Otley. On one or two weekends when there were no parades I hopped on the small Sammy Ledgards bus to Leeds, as did several others. We soon learned to dodge the two Military Policemen (MPs) at the Cookridge Street terminus, by getting off a stop earlier. I was never caught without a leave pass, always making it back to camp before 10pm and 'lights out'.

Chapter 8

In early February 1945 my left knee, which had occasionally given trouble since Cyprus, finally gave up on me. On reporting sick I was promptly packed off to Leeds Infirmary to see the consultant Mr Pain and to be x-rayed. Back at the camp I was put on light duties at the cookhouse - spud-peeling and washing up. Scarcely believing my luck two weeks later I was taken to Pinderfields Hospital for removal of a cystic cartilage, and put in E ward - which I had actually helped to build early in 1940. The whole (supposedly temporary) wing was now given over to forces' casualties, except one ward which was for mining accidents. I felt a complete fraud being there as most of the others were battlefront casualties. Some with horrific wounds - mainly from the invasion front which by that time was over the Rhine and advancing rapidly into Germany.

The atmosphere in the ward was certainly not downhearted, as victory was in sight, but the ward building would have given today's health and safety people nightmares. In freezing winter weather the total heating came from two ancient coke-burning stoves, placed at each end of the ward. Considering the actual structure this was totally inadequate. The outer wall was a single 4 ½-inch thick coke breeze block, with small brick strengthening pillars every four yards, separated by outwards opening single-glazed metal-framed French windows around the whole building. The same basic structure, with many improvements, still exists today - 63 years later. Two wards were demolished to be replaced by a modern two storey block - for which I can vouch as being first class, having recently been a patient there.

A totally new hospital which was promised so many years ago is in sight. The military wing was classed as temporary with a maximum life of 10 years when I built it! In spite of the poor working conditions, the nursing staff were marvellous, with a strict matron in charge of each ward. On the 15th February my cartilage was removed by Mr. Pain, who came just one day per week from Leeds General Infirmary. I awoke to find a light alloy splint, 18-inches long, strapped to the back of my leg to prevent the knee from bending. This stayed in place for the following four weeks until I was discharged.

One good thing was having Nora able to visit in the evenings after work as she lived only a mile away. The same operation today would probably mean only two days in hospital, but with my knee stubbornly refusing to bend and, in spite of daily therapy, it was a total of 12-weeks. Towards the end of April I was graded A1 fit to return to full duty and discharged but ever since I have never had full mobility in the knee. Two weeks after the operation, like other walking-wounded, I was allowed into town with a stiff-legged limp, dressed in hospital blue jacket and trousers, white shirt and red tie - by now a common sight around town. We were only allowed out until 8pm but it was easy to enter the ward at 10pm by avoiding the main gate and walking in the back way via Long Causeway, as it's still known. I could then slip through the purposely unlocked French window beside my bed. The staff would conveniently turn a blind eye. The last four weeks, with the splint removed were happy ones. I was free to go out every day after physiotherapy and spend every evening and weekends from about 1pm with Nora - going to the cinema two or three times a week and doing plenty of walking.

One week I was given leave from the hospital and Nora managed to get leave from work on 'compassionate grounds', so we took off for Blackpool, on what we called a very belated honeymoon. Although still very cold, it was really enjoyable – we stayed in a small guest house with no other guests. The very kind owners allowed us to dine with them.

I was then sent to another convalescent and re-habilitation camp for ex-POWs, who were returning in large numbers from the liberated German camps. This one was at Holmfield Park, Ovenden, near Halifax and the routine here was similar to Otley, but more advanced. Several 7th Green Howards men arrived from Germany, captured like me on 29th June '42. So we had much to talk about, including the fate of the 9,000 inmates of Camp 70, who at the Italian Armistice were quickly scooped up by the Germans and packed on to trains to Austria and Germany. They were subjected to a horrific journey of several days' without food in cattle trucks. This made me realise how very lucky I had been not to suffer the same fate. So much for General Montgomery's futile order to 'stand fast' and await liberation. A very few did ignore the order and, assisted by friendly civilians, got through the German lines to safety. One of these was our own Colonel McDonnell who made it dressed as a woman. Freddie Hindle, my

old desert comrade, turned up - telling me he had been elected
'British man of confidence' in a large German camp, which
meant a man elected by his fellow prisoners, to try to win better
conditions and food from the Germans.

Although we were officially restricted to the Halifax area in off-
duty time, I managed to get home several evenings in the first
three week as we were free after 4.00pm until the following day's
parade - there were no evening roll calls or any other checks. I
discovered from several others that the best way to get further
afield was to avoid the railway station where sometimes two MPs
(military police - not the politician variety) would be looking for
men without a leave pass. Although the camp was surrounded
by barbed wire it was easy to crawl underneath at the rear and
run across the Halifax to Keighley road to a bus stop. To go then
from Keighley to Leeds and then Wakefield - being home about
6.00pm; returning by a late through train and then plodding up
the hill to Ovendon.

One night I was about to ascend the steps from the platform to
the exit when I spotted the two MPs checking on someone else.
I did a smart u-turn, helped by the very dim lighting and walked
off the platform end on to the track-side into near total darkness.
I walked on, looking for a possible exit, when an elderly railway
man appeared, swinging his lamp and wanting to know what I
was up to. He must have had a soft heart because he led me to
a small gate which opened on to the road. The inevitable was
bound to happen and my luck ran out at the weekend prior to
the announcement of VE day (Victory in Europe) after the
German surrender.

The only weekend duty was to attend Sunday morning church
parade with numbers being checked by Corporal Bourne who
was in charge of the hut. On the Saturday he promised to mark
me present - allowing me a whole weekend at home but for
some reason someone else had checked the numbers and I was

marked absent. This led to an AWOL (Absent Without Leave) charge and on Monday morning I was marched smartly by the camp sergeant-major and flanked by two other men into the Commanding Officer's office, who gave me a severe dressing down and seven days' CB (confined to barracks). Even knowing I had done wrong it was still humiliating to think that, after five years service with an unblemished record, I was punished for a minor offence. He also added, "If you go absent again, I'll see to it you'll be behind bars again". I could have spoken up with "I was never literally behind bars sir", but that would have earned me another seven days for being insolent.

The next day, Tuesday 8th May, everyone else who was near enough went home for the day but the few of us doing CB were put on cook-house fatigues scrubbing pots, pans and tables - and fuming at missing the day's celebrations. The following day my sentence, along with the others, was quashed by the pompous CO - so once more I had a crime-free record.

A few days later, along with several others, I was passed fit for all duties, which also meant the possibility of overseas service again. First we needed a period of intensive training - effectively becoming recruits. We were soon under escort on a train to Scotland. First we went to Glasgow and then a further 20 miles north to Alexandria, Dunbartonshire, arriving at what was then known as Bonhill Barracks. This was a large stone-built grim-looking building, occupied by officers and NCOs of the 9th Battalion Bedfordshire and Hertfordshire Regiment. They were there to take ex-POWs through the recruit training course, which was to last about 10 weeks. Here the main emphasis was on physical fitness and, like Otley, more weapon training - although we were still not issued with personal weapons. There were more lectures and visits to various locations, mainly on the west coast, to watch demonstrations of the latest artillery guns and tanks - such as the Flail, for destroying land mines and the powerful new American tanks. There were route marches and cross-country runs and sessions in the gym. This was equipped with very high scramble nets which we had to climb up one side and then down the other.

During this period Nora was granted two weeks compassionate leave from work to visit me, but the journey proved to be quite an ordeal, with the train being packed, as was the norm in wartime and she had to stand all the way to Glasgow. As it was a Saturday I was able to meet her off the train, to her immense relief. I obtained a sleeping-out pass for two weeks and managed to find accommodation in a nice bungalow in the village of Balloch, at the southern end of Loch Lomond - just a mile from the barracks. I had been hoping that Freddie Hindle would be in my group to leave Otley but he wasn't fit enough, and was discharged from the army shortly afterwards. Although we never met again, we did correspond for a while.

One man from our old 18 Platoon during Castle Cary days was Cyril (Jeff) Jefferson, one of those released from a German camp. His home was in Bridlington and he had got married on the long leave. He also had Evelyn, his wife, lodged in Balloch - so she and Nora were able to be together during the day with all of us meeting up in the evening. We were always allowed into Glasgow in free time - it being only a half-hour train journey away. Loch Lomond park was nearby and, with lovely fine and warm evenings, it was very pleasant in the park. There were also rowing boats, at which I was a bit of a dunce – I think I scared Nora!

The second week of Nora's visit saw the true end of the war - with the Japanese surrender and 8th August was declared VJ Day. Nora and I were given the news late on the previous evening after we had gone to bed - being awakened by the family's daughter. There was very little sleep that night! The 8th dawned to pouring rain, which lasted most of the day. Upon returning to barracks we were given the day off, so it was straight back to Balloch to collect the girls and take the next train to Glasgow - spending a large part of the day in Greens' Playhouse Ballroom, a famous wartime venue, with one of the top bands always in attendance. After this it was back to the training routine with Nora needing to return home.

At the barracks there were rumours that we would soon be drafted out to the Far East to join the occupation forces, allowing some of the battle weary troops to return home. Around the end of August, with the course nearing its end, we were told that when possible, we would be returned to our own units. It was a few days later that Jeff and I and a few others would be re-joining the 7th Green Howards in East Yorkshire, in the Pickering area.

Fig 21 - Jim and Margaret Mason

Our old 'D' Company was at Kirbymoorside and Battalion HQ at Thornton-le-Dale. They had been brought back from the continent after being at the forefront of the battles for several months after D-Day. So, a few days later after three years absence, we were back with the battalion and 'D' Company and billeted in two Nissen huts by the roadside in Kirbymoorside, with a small cook-house attached. Apart from Jeff and me there was Frank Shepherd, also from Bonhill. Most of the other men were new to us except Sergeant Stan 'Westy' Westmoreland, who later married a Kirby schoolteacher, Jim Mason, RQMS at Battalion HQ and surprisingly Colonel MacDonnell, who was back as CO after his escape. The daily routine was very relaxed - just the usual morning PT, drill and road running - having finally being re-armed with rifles. Several afternoons in the next few weeks were free time and we were allowed into Scarborough - a welcome diversion.

Around the middle of September, news came that the battalion was to be given the freedom of Bridlington in honour of its fine war record. It was formed here before the war as a Territorial Army unit. This led to extra drill parades to ready us for the big occasion, which was to take place on the first weekend in October. I believe it was at the end of the second practice, while waiting to be dismissed, that the sergeant major shouted, "Is there a Manton on parade?" No one answered when immediately it hit me, 'could it be me?' On telling him my name I was sent to the office for confirmation. The duty officer said "I have information here that your civilian occupation was bricklayer and as there is now an urgent need in the country for building tradesmen, you are being offered the chance of early release to work in your home area". General demobilisation was already taking place by numbered groups. My number was 31 and was not eligible for a further nine months - number 25 group going at that time. So I had no hesitation in accepting. I was told in no uncertain terms it would be a Class-B Release. This meant I could be recalled in the event of another emergency, as opposed to Class-A which was a permanent release. With the prospect of another overseas posting, I felt I had surely made the right decision. There was another emergency during the Suez Crisis, in 1956, but I wasn't called-up.

After the good news I could hardly wait to let Nora know, so I went straight to the post office to send her a telegram. Further good news was it could take effect immediately. On the following day to I had to hand in all my equipment and go to York to the demobilisation clothing depot to be fitted out, although I was allowed to keep my uniform and greatcoat - which came in very useful at work in the cold post-war winters. Jeff was in 25 group so we were able to travel together, taking the clothing in large cardboard boxes back to Kirby. Next stop was the office to collect discharge papers, three weeks' pay and ration cards and £70. This is what was known as a gratuity and paid according to length of service. I only took one week's holiday before starting work as we needed every penny to set up our own home.

On the last night in our billet we were given no rest, being dragged out of bed, sleepless, with all the friendly horseplay and so to the final day - 27th September 1945 after five years and three months and supremely glad to be going home. Jeff and I parted company in York - he caught a train to Bridlington and I got one to Wakefield, going back to all the post-war shortages.

Having been so lucky to survive to our late eighties, Nora and I were never to be blessed with children. This was partly because, in our younger days, there wasn't the fertility treatment available today - but we're very content with all our memories, and very happy to have survived so long and very content in our sheltered bungalow.

Nora's Story

Chapter 1

This is my story, which is not quite so exciting as John's, but in many ways a similarly tough childhood as I was born in the immediate aftermath of the First World War at Blenheim Road Maternity Hospital, Wakefield. This was a time when all working class families were struggling to make a living and to put food on the table.

Fig 22 - Nora, aged 16.

My dad, John Watson, was a coalminer working at Parkhills Colliery, on the east side of Wakefield. Mine workers in the 1920's were among the lowest paid in the country, so it was always a struggle to survive. Being on the regular night shift at the pit he also did some gardening work. This was mainly for the family doctor, Dr Greaves, whose home and surgery was a large very old detached dwelling on the site which later became the NHS Pricing Bureau. Incidentally this was where our niece was later to work. Later still the site became part of the Ridings Shopping Centre and Boots the Chemists.

My mother, Elizabeth Ellis, married in 1913 and had her first child, Jack, in 1915. At that time they were living in Kilby Street which runs along the north side of St. John's Square and the Church. We lived in a block of four back-to-back, 'one up - one down' cottages, with the backyard containing the toilet block. I came along on the 29th January 1921 in what was then Wakefield Maternity Home - one of several large detached houses in Blenheim Road, which runs off the start of Leeds Road in St John's. Mother said she was annoyed with me for coming into the world at lunchtime consequently missing her meal! On being taken home I started bawling and big brother Jack, then aged five, shouted, in proper Yorkshire dialect, "Tek 'er back t' terny 'ome!" - so much for brotherly love! Being only two years of age at the time, I have no recollection of the birth of my younger brother, Eric in 1923.

I grew up a sickly child but, at four years old, I started at St. John's Girls School. I remember Mother taking me on my first day, she was wheeling Eric in a very large perambulator which was then the usual conveyance for a baby. The school was in Clarendon Street, in the College Grove area, a half-mile from home. This was quite a walk for a small girl but there was hardly any problem crossing roads in those days with very little traffic. I also did the walk at lunchtime. Later, when Eric was old enough for school, he was fortunate in only having to walk to St. John's

Fig 23: Nora's mother, Elizabeth

Boys School which was just at the end of Kilby Street. Jack later
went to Thornes House Secondary School, which in those days
was the equivalent of a grammar school. He had passed the
County Minor Scholarship Test at the eligible age of 11 years and
transferred from St. John's in 1926.

127

Eric and I tended to play together, being closer in age. Older brother Jack had his own friends of a similar age. Later, when old enough not to need my company, Eric found his own school pals for playmates. I had several friends - getting up to the usual childish mischief. There was Minnie Newby, Joan Kellet, Winnie Smith and Nora Osborne. One of our play areas was an old disused greenhouse where we made mud pies and put them to bake in a small tank, resting on a high shelf. One day I was reaching up to put my pies in the oven, and pulled the whole lot down on top of me, gashing my forehead. Another time while walking to school, I fell on a broken bottle. I gashed my knee, which should really have been stitched but it wasn't so I still have the scar.

A popular pastime was to walk down through an area, then known as the cabbage gardens - a council owned allotment site alongside the main Leeds to London railway. You could walk through a tunnel beneath the line, then follow a path heading towards Wrenthorpe village and come across another path which led to Alverthorpe - forming a kind of crossroads. At this intersection stood a miniature sewage works, known as the filter-beds. Just across the second path from there and running alongside was a swampy ditch containing smelly effluent. Maybe you've already guessed but one day, accident prone me fell in. My playmate, Winnie Shearman, who lived in a St. John's North flat with a bathroom, took me there for a good wash down. Someone else had let Mother know and she came to take me home and I was lucky to be let off lightly with no punishment. It wasn't all playtime - often before school I would run into town to shop for Mother and our neighbours, mostly for food - which earned me a few coppers.

Jack left school in 1931 at the height of the industrial depression years with perhaps three million unemployed. I don't remember exactly when but he eventually started work at a small garage in

Andrew Street, St. Johns. By this time we had moved to a larger two bedroomed house in York Place, just off Northgate, near the top of York Street with the toilet still outside. Eventually Jack found a more permanent job at Greens Engineering Works.

In my pre-teen years, I suffered a serious illness and was confined to bed for quite a long period. I eventually made a good recovery but I had missed out on a lot of education and was glad to be able to leave school, aged 14. I soon found a job at Ralph Bell's Lemonade Works in Kirkgate. The pay was five shillings per week (25 pence today) for washing out dirty bottles but I resigned after only one week - wet through and with sore hands from unscrewing the bottle tops. My next job was also in Kirkgate at Lee's small bakery which had an attached café. I helped with washing-up and other odd jobs and was given a good meal at lunchtime. I don't remember why but I soon left the café and went to work at George Lees Woollen Mill at Westgate End. This was demolished along with Ings Road School a few years ago to make way for the new Westgate Retail Park. The work was winding the wool into hanks, on a piece-work basis - which meant the more we did the larger wage we earned.

At about this time the family moved again - to 31 Hope Street. This time it was to a large terrace house with a cellar, kitchen and an extra attic bedroom. The house still stands but part of the street was demolished to make way for the Lightwaves Swimming Baths. Jack and his friend, Ronnie Appleyard, had formed a small, spare time dance band, with Jack on drums. They used our cellar for practice sessions, eventually played at the Embassy Ballroom in Market Street and around the clubs. Ronnie's family had a jewellery business in Westgate.

Eric left school in 1937 and, being an enthusiastic gardener - having helped Dad with his spare time gardening work, was given work along with Cecil Wales, his friend, in the grounds of what was then known as the Bishop's residence. For many years since this has been the Bishopsgarth police training college. Eric and Cecil were both confirmed by the bishop during their time there.

I had a workmate called Dorothy Margison and we used to go out together, as did most teenagers. This was mostly at weekends when it was either to the cinema or parading round town - chatting to boys. We had a good choice of cinemas, back then there was the Regal, Empire, Carlton, Electric and Playhouse.

This was also the time of gathering war clouds, with Hitler ranting and raving and our government, under Prime Minister Chamberlain, doing their best to appease him, all ultimately to no avail. The storm broke on 3rd September 1939, and we were then at war. In the early months there wasn't much change in daily life, except for the almost blacked out streets with only an occasional very dim street lamp. We carried on with the same work at the mill - but it was an ordeal walking there morning and night in almost total darkness.

From about 16 years of age, Dorothy and I had learned to dance, mostly at the Unity Hall and the Embassy. We stopped at the start of the war - it would have meant walking home late and alone. Dad always insisted I was home by 10pm, so it was usually just a trip to the cinema on Saturday evenings, often queuing in the cold to get in and sometimes having to stand in the aisles through the whole programme. A small fairground managed to keep operating alongside the outdoor market area, with just a couple of rides and a few dimly lit stalls. This came to an end in 1940, with the high risk of air-raids.

Fig 24 (opposite):
Nora, aged 18

Chapter 2

One Saturday evening - November 11th 1939, Dorothy and I went to the Carlton cinema. We then had a look at the fair and started to walk back into Upper Kirkgate and, whilst crossing The Springs, almost collided with two lads with who we started chatting - in the middle of the road with no traffic about. They didn't seem to be the usual run-of-the-mill chatter-uppers. They wore smart raincoats and kid gloves and they must have made a good impression on us as we all arranged to meet on the following Saturday - Len to take Dorothy and John with me. Dorothy probably thought Len, who was a very good looking lad with curly ginger hair, to have seemed a bit too 'la-di-dah' posh for her and I don't think any romance blossomed.

This was not so with John and me - it was more like the words of a lovely song of the day, 'Love in Bloom' - sung by Jessie Matthews in the film 'Evergreen'. After going to the cinema on our first date, John walked me home. As there was a most convenient narrow passage between our house, number 31, and number 33 next door, we could 'canoodle' for a while before John had to set off to walk home to Wrenthorpe – but not before arranging to meet again the next weekend.

Complications arose when Dorothy, who was always a bit bossy with me, insisted I should continue going out with her at weekends and see John during the week. Of course softy me, not being able to contradict her, agreed and John was happy to take me out on Tuesday evenings. After a week or two and our romance progressing nicely I plucked up courage and told Dorothy I wanted to be with John more. From then on she turned very cool towards me. Shortly after this she was conscripted to work at the Barnbow munitions factory outside Leeds. After the war she got married and emigrated to Canada but I don't think she ever forgave me for going my own way.

John then started coming for me four times in the week and we really enjoyed ourselves. One Saturday night, he was about to set off home, when Dad came to the door and said to John, in his best Yorkshire accent, "Cum in lad, let's 'ave a look at thee", and from then onwards our relationship was cemented. Our Jack had already been courting Amy Posliff for a good while before the war and they had got used to having a little privacy in our front room on Saturday evenings but they very kindly allowed John and me to do the same on alternate weeks - a whole lot better than being outside on the cold winter nights.

John's friend Len, then just 18 years old, volunteered for the RAF in spite of having good career prospects with Stanley Council, studying to be a sanitary inspector. He was accepted to undertake air-crew training in Wales. This had caused John to think the same way, knowing he would be conscripted on his 20th birthday in April 1940. Having passed the medical in Leeds, he was rejected for not having sat for his Grammar School Certificate but was offered Balloon Barrage Training - which he refused. Early in the New Year, having a trade as a bricklayer, he tried for the Royal Engineers but was told he was 'too young - come back when you are 20.' So he decided to just wait for the call-up, whenever it might be.

I don't remember much about that first wartime Christmas, except it was very cold, with all food and clothing being rationed - a coupon system operated. Christmas Day was on a Monday that year, so everyone was only allowed that day and Boxing Day as holiday from work, which in any case had been the norm for years before that, with no holiday pay for most. I remember the weather being very cold which went into the New Year. John was working on the emergency extension at the Pinderfields Hospital site, in readiness for the expected service casualties from the continent. We continued to be together as much as possible. I was still walking to and from work during the blackout but nearly always accompanied by two or three neighbours who were doing the same work.

In spring, just a few days after his birthday, John received notice to go to Huddersfield for a medical and was passed grade A1 fit for military service. So we knew that inevitably he would be called up soon. Meanwhile what had been known as the 'phoney war', due to only the Air Force and Navy seeing action, hotted up. The Germans skirting round the supposedly impregnable Maginot Line and driving forward into Belgium and France. Six weeks later saw the start of a general evacuation of the British Army, after suffering many casualties, through the Channel port of Dunkirk. This meant that although 358,000 troops got safely home many Units needed to be reinforced, especially the Infantry and John became one of the enlisted reinforcements.

On Monday 10th June John received an order to report to the famous Green Howards Yorkshire Regiment Depot at Richmond, North Yorkshire on the 13th June for eight weeks basic infantry training. The next morning he gave notice at work and received his full due wages. When he came to me in the evening we decided to get engaged and, because the shops stayed open till 8pm, we went off to Harland's Jewellers (opposite Woolworths and now a bookies) and, we bought my ring out of his final wage packet. Happily I am still wearing it almost 70 years later. Afterwards we nipped across the road to the Regal cinema to watch Judy Garland in 'The Wizard of Oz'.

Wednesday evening brought tearful farewells - us having no idea what the future held for us and looking back now, in some ways, no bad thing. The whole country, after Dunkirk, was in a state of emergency, expecting the Germans to come pouring across the Channel to invade us. It was only the RAF which prevented that happening by beating the German Air Force in what became 'The Battle of Britain'.

Jack married Amy on the 15th June 1940. Jack was exempted from military service as he had been struck down with rheumatic fever in his teenage years spending three weeks seriously ill in Clayton Hospital. He was working at Green's Engineering Works where the firm was producing war materials and so most of the employees were exempt and classed as being in a Reserved Occupation.

John and I had to be content with letter-writing as often as possible with no chance of an early leave for him. The training was hard with long days but he probably endured it better than some others who had been used to office work and similar whilst

Fig 25:
Nora's brother, Jack and his wife, Amy
on their wedding day - 15th June 1940

he had been used to hard physical work in the building trade. Much of my leisure time besides helping Mother with housework and shopping was spent bike-riding in the summer months with my friend Joan Kellet and, of course, missing John terribly.

By the middle of August, with the Battle of Britain being fought in the skies over southern England and having completed the basic training, John was posted with several others to the 7th Battalion Green Howards. They had returned from Dunkirk and needed reinforcements - the headquarters was at Wimborne, Dorset and the Green Howard Companys were put on coast defence in the Bournemouth-Poole area. John was sent to D-Company, covering the Sandbanks stretch of coast. This is now home to several celebrity millionaires and one of the most expensive property areas in the world. Back then it was a case of digging trenches on the beach and waiting for the expected invasion.

In late October, with the threat of invasion having receded, the Company was given leave and John arrived at our house one evening. He was heavily laden with all his kit, equipment, and rifle after an unbelievable 22-hour rail journey from Bournemouth, having travelled at a restricted 15 miles per hour to London because of the bombing. This was followed by several hours delay in London because of air-raid alerts. The reason they had to carry all their kit was because the Battalion was to be moved during that week to a training area at Castle Cary, near Yeovil, Somerset. Mother and Dad, knowing of John's unhappy home life, allowed him to stay with us. During this leave he went home for some of his belongings but said his Dad had not been at all happy with our arrangement although there was nothing he could do about it.

In effect, the seven days leave was only five because the last one was spent in return travel. John now had a new friend, Jim Mason, who had a further two hours travel to his home in Horton-in-Ribblesdale near Settle. Jim and his future wife became our lifelong friends - more of that later.

In the first week of January, they were given a further leave. Their journey proved to be slightly quicker - travelling via Bristol instead of London and this time they were not burdened like pack mules. Jim and Margaret were engaged like us. They got married during that leave. It was so good to be together again, if only for a few short days. I still had to go to work, however, which seemed to make the time together pass even quicker.

In late February I sensed something unpleasant was happening to John, and indeed his next letter said he had been very ill after being exposed to bitter weather on all-night training schemes on Exmoor in Devon. The good thing was he got sick leave for a week, so we were given an unexpected lovely few days together. This was the same week in March when bombs were dropped on Wakefield, resulting in several deaths. They were also dropped on Leeds - with many more killed.

After that leave it became obvious, following intensive training, that John's unit would be moving abroad. It was most likely this would be to the Middle East where battles were being fought in the North African Campaign. Sure enough, on Saturday 5th April, he was home again on what became known as embarkation leave.

Arriving home at 6.00am, he suggested seeing if it was possible to be married in so short a time. I readily agreed to this and, after breakfast, we went to see the vicar of St. John's Church, explaining that we had only got till Thursday 10th April. After trying to put us off with several excuses, like "you're too young", he saw we were determined and agreed to marry us on Monday the 7th at 11.00am. A special licence was essential, as was a signed statement from our parents allowing the wedding to take place. This was because we were both under 21 - John was only four days short and I was nine months short.

This meant a frantic dash for both of us. John was lucky - the Registry Office was open till noon, and he got the licence, which I think cost £3. He managed to locate his dad, who was working on a surface air-raid shelter in West Parade and obtained his signed statement. For my part, mother and I did a quick tour of the shops and found it difficult to find anything suitable. I had to be satisfied with a green mixture costume and hat, which I never really liked, and black shoes, using all my coupons and some of mother's. On the Sunday evening, John left to spend the night at the home of cousin Elsie and her husband, Mo, who lived at Westgate End. Monday morning found us at the Church for 11.00am prompt.

Most of our two families were not allowed time off work to attend, so there was only Elsie and Mo, John's sister Millie and my parents. After the wedding we went back to our house where we had only been able to get a plain cake and some wine. That didn't matter to us as we knew we had achieved what we most wanted - that is to become married. I was not even allowed time off work until Thursday, when John had to leave and so it was back to work for me the morning after the wedding.

Then came the moment we were dreading - 9.00pm on 10th April and, with snow beginning to fall on platform 1 at Westgate Station, we had a tearful parting. John had to catch the southbound troop train in York. I cried on the walk home, having no idea when I would see my husband again, if ever. I knew I was not alone in this as it was happening to thousands of others all over the country. Our only contact at this time was by letter-writing.

Fig 25: Nora's brother, Eric, in Italy in the RASC

Chapter 3

Having been issued with tropical kit it was obvious John's unit was heading for warmer climes and they left Gourock on the Clyde on 3rd June under tight security. I didn't know this at the time and it was many weeks before I got another letter. Whilst in England John had heard of a simple code he could use in his letters – so he could at least tell me which country he was in. We created a list of all the countries we could think of and attached a boy or girls name to each one. He would ask in his letters if 'so-and-so' was all right and, with me having the list it worked very well.

Fig 26: John's brother, Eric, in the RASC

Eric had, by now, left the Bishop's residence. He trained as a wood machinist at Drake and Waters, a well known timber manufacturing firm and his friend, Cecil, had gone to work in a hardware shop. With the conscription age being lowered from 20 years to 18, Eric was called into the RASC (Royal Army Service Corps) in the latter half of 1941. By coincidence my brother, Eric, and John's identically-named brother found themselves in the same draft - doing their basic training and later a driving course in Sheffield together. My brother was sent out to Italy, having been medically graded A1. He thankfully returned safely at the end of the war. John's brother was graded B2 and was sent to HQ Eastern Command, being able to follow his trade as a plumber for part of his remaining service time.

I now want to talk a little about my work. I think it was in late 1941 that woollen manufacture was suspended at Lees. The RAF took over the building to use it as their clothing depot - supplying new items to the many new emergency airfields springing up throughout Yorkshire and beyond. Second-hand clothing was also sorted for possible re-use - this became my job along with those others who had not been sent to work on munitions. I also had phone work to do - which meant ringing round the various airfields to persuade them to send what they could. At times this work became stressful with some of the items being blood-stained, them having coming from shot-down air-crews. The work was supervised by RAF officers. One of them told me I should address him as 'Sir' but the usually timid me stood up to him, "I'm not in the services," I said - and refused to do so.

Stonehouses Mill, which stood just across the road from Lees, was also taken over for the same work later in the war. I was moved there and I had to do even more phone work - which I never really liked.

We all had to learn to deal with the possibility of incendiary bombs being dropped. This was done at Hayley's Mill on Alverthorpe Road. It was there that we fire-watched in twos on all night stints. No bombs were dropped in that area but they were dropped on Thornes Road, Belle Vue and Wrenthorpe.

Some weekends, weather permitting, I used to go biking with my friend, Joan, who had relations living in Sheffield. One Saturday night there was a heavy raid in Sheffield and hundreds were killed. Joan decided to go there on the Sunday to see if her relations were all right. I went along for what proved to be a scary ride. I think the distance is about 28-miles. Soon after setting out on the return trip around tea-time Joan got her front wheel jammed firmly in a tram line. She told me to carry on and not stop for anyone - as it was already approaching dusk. Although being really scared I managed to get home all right. Joan was helped by a passer-by, who deflated the tyre, which released the wheel, and blew the tyre up again - she didn't catch me up though. Fortunately, there was hardly any traffic on the roads, it being a Sunday. On another long Sunday ride Joan and I went to Wetherby. In 1944 a large glider force was assembling on the racecourse prior to the airborne drop at Arnhem.

We were allowed a few days summer holiday from work and I had started corresponding with Jim Mason's wife, Margaret. Twice she invited me to stay at their home in Horton-in-Ribblesdale - the lovely Yorkshire Dales village. I enjoyed some lovely bike rides with Margaret, with plenty to talk about - us both being newly-weds.

All mail was heavily censored, and most letters were two or three weeks in transit but through our little code I was able to keep track on John's movements. This was useful with the battalion constantly on the move around the Middle East. Early in 1942, the letters became fewer and contained very little real information

ig 27: Christmas greeting
nt by John whilst in Palestine

- although by using the code we knew they were in the Libyan Desert Battle and therefore feared for their safety. From May onwards the actual war news got steadily worse - culminating in the big retreat hundreds of miles back into Egypt, and the loss of the port of Tobruk for the second time.

Having received no letters from John for a long time I became really worried for him. I don't think we realised at home what was really happening on the battlefront - as all news was strictly censored. The 8th Army was in full retreat - trying to reach El Alamein, the last fortified defence line before Cairo, Alexandria, and the vast oil-fields of all the Middle East. John's battalion (or what was left of it after the May/June battles at Gazala) had about 300 troops left from a full strength of 800 to 900. It was ordered to form a delaying line about 20 miles west of Alamein - without prepared defences. Along with the remnants of the whole army and with barely any armoured support it was doomed to failure when the enemy's armoured columns caught up.

John remembers losing track of Jim during the Gazala evacuation. Jim joining the column which headed south, then east - and John going north, then east down the coast road. When they met again and seeing Jim in such a poor state lying propped up against their truck wheel with stomach pains, John managed to scrounge him a mug of tea. That was the last John saw of him for a while. Jim managed to join a few other stragglers and reach Alamein. Two and a half years passed before they met again - in happier circumstances.

At home five very worrying months passed between John's last letter and a War Office letter arriving telling us he was a prisoner in Italy, the camp not known. It was a further few weeks before a very small single page arrived - which just told me he was well and the address at Camp 70. He was not being allowed to say any more. A not very happy Christmas came with just two days of holiday otherwise walking to the still unpleasant work in cold blacked-out streets.

Over the next several months I received more of the special single-page letters with only the permitted phrases. Articles of food and clothing could be sent back - these had a weight limit and became known as personal parcels. Although I sent several over much of 1943, John only remembers receiving the first one - so there must have been much pilfering in transit.

Around midsummer, a letter said he had joined a group to go out to work and that he was in Transit Camp Number 62, at Bergamo in north Italy. Small groups were sent out from here, mainly to farms, but his group had different work – which is described in his story.

The Italian capitulation came on 8th September, the news giving me hope that he might soon be set free. My hopes soon faded when the Germans quickly took control of the camps and the Italian army. The Germans sent trainloads of prisoners up through the Brenner Pass to further imprisonment in German and Austrian camps. There was news of one train being bombed on the way, with much loss of life and once again all the old worries returned for me - fearing again for John's safety. This started another horrible period with five months silence after his last letter.

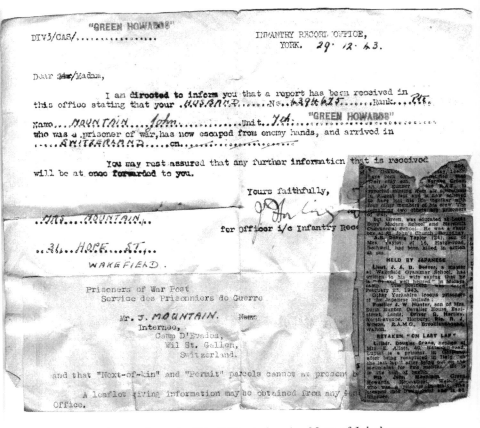

Fig 28: Telegram from the War Office informing Nora of John's escape.

Chapter 4

By Christmas there was still no news when, out of the blue on 29th December, a War Office telegram arrived notifying us John had escaped and was safe in Switzerland. This gave me joyful hope of soon having him home. However mail was still very slow - taking two to three weeks - and still heavily censored. John couldn't say anything about his escape although I knew from his address that all his time there was spent in the north-east of the country. He was able to tell me about being involved with a practical basic building course - teaching others his bricklaying knowledge. In the summer he went off with another bricklayer to work for a Swiss building firm on two sites - keeping his hand in and preparing for future work after the war.

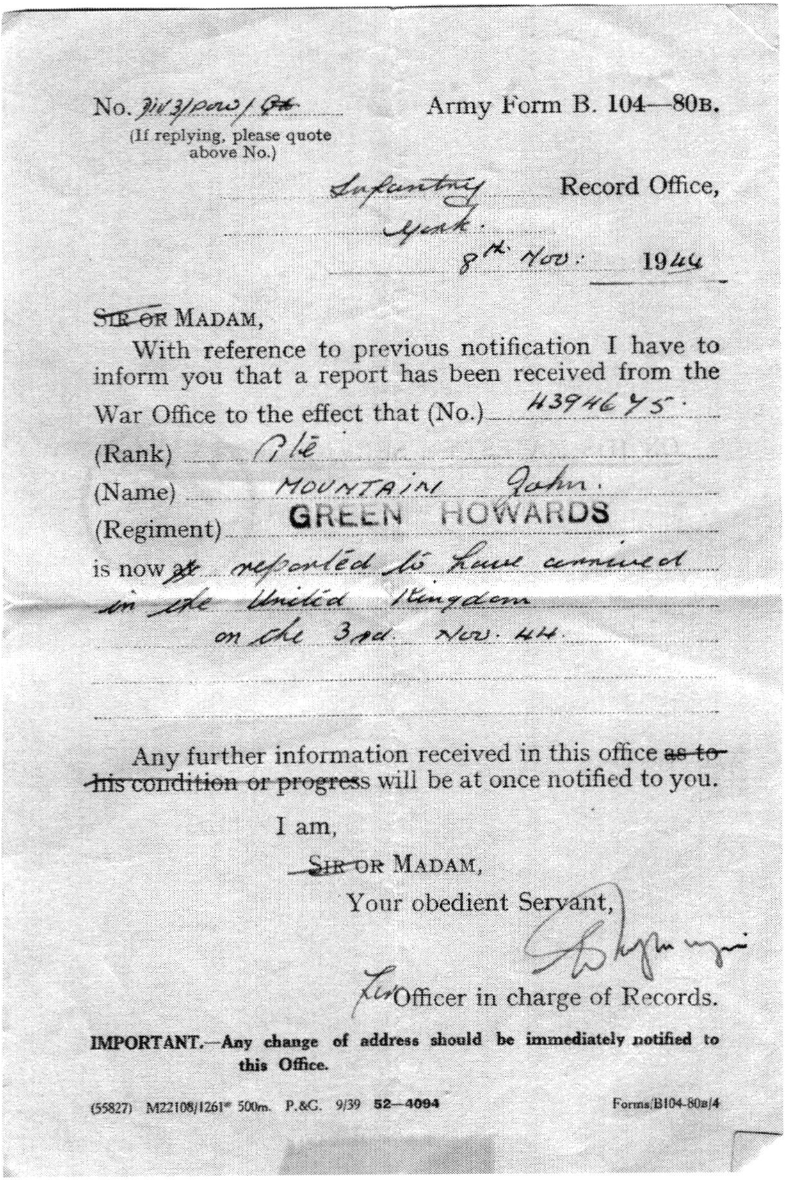

No. *3103/pow/G#*   Army Form B. 104—80B.
(If replying, please quote
        above No.)

Infantry   Record Office,

York.

8th Nov.   19*44*

SIR OR MADAM,

With reference to previous notification I have to
inform you that a report has been received from the
War Office to the effect that (No.) *4394675.*

(Rank) *Ple*

(Name) *MOUNTAIN   John.*

(Regiment) GREEN HOWARDS

is now ~~at~~ *reported to have arrived
in the United Kingdom
on the 3rd. Nov. 44.*

Any further information received in this office ~~as to~~
~~his condition or progress~~ will be at once notified to you.

I am,

SIR OR MADAM,

Your obedient Servant,

Officer in charge of Records.

IMPORTANT.—Any change of address should be immediately notified to
this Office.

(55827) M22108/1261ᵉ 500m. P.&G. 9/39 **52—4094**   Forms/B104-80a/4

Fig 29: Telegram from War Office notifying Nora of John's arrival in the UK

At home rationing got even worse with long queues outside the shops in all weathers - supermarkets were unheard of then. Food was the worst problem; my mother would stand for hours and I also did so when I was able. Shops would often be sold out before we got in, despite us having coupons. Particularly upsetting was the fact that we had used precious coupons to make up several parcels for John with only the first one reaching him.

On a lighter note, John's brother, Eric, while on leave from the Army, took me to the Embassy. One evening a competition was held for the best couple in each dance. Eric and I came second in the 'fox-trot'. John never did learn to dance; his sister, Millie, offered to take him after he left school but his Dad wouldn't allow it - probably thinking he might be led astray by staying out late. It's hard to imagine these days but that was the way some parents thought then.

So now, back to my story!

The invasion of the continent came on 6th June, with John's unit being among the first to land on 'Gold Beach' and a VC being won on the first day. Jim Mason was, however, one of only a very few left of the original battalion. From then on the war news was nearly all good but it was distressing for Wakefield people to see train loads of wounded arriving at Westgate station – on their way to Pinderfields Hospital. We soon got used to seeing the more able ones walking in town in their blue uniforms.

Although John's letters were coming regularly during the summer it was always all fairly old news and nothing concerning the war - due to censoring by British officer escapees. There was no hint of when he might be coming home. If the Germans had invaded Switzerland, which throughout the war had been a constant threat, all the ex-prisoners would have had to join the Swiss Army in their mountain redoubt. This was something I didn't know about until he finally did come home.

Fig 30: John's despatch notice for passage to the UK

John was able to tell me how he was enjoying his work in the lovely weather, with good food and lodging but wasn't allowed to say that as soon as the Allies reached the Swiss border, they would be able to leave. I think the last letter I received was dated early October. I didn't know on receiving it that he was already at sea, well on the way home.

On 4th November John was able to send a telegram from Amersham, Buckinghamshire to say he expected to come home the following day. On the 5th, without the traditional bonfires - there still being a slight risk of air-raids, he walked in at tea-time. The years of anxiety and tears were finally at an end. I can only repeat how John has lovingly described those wonderful first moments of re-union, relief and happiness, never to be forgotten throughout our long lives.

Much as I wished otherwise, work had to go on – there was no let up on the amount of clothing to be dealt with. The RAF were still heavily engaged over on the continent and having casualties. One was Len Hartley and as soon as we could, we went to visit his parents in Wrenthorpe. Len's mother was just coming down Silcoates Hill, where they lived. On seeing us she broke down, weeping in her grief, a heart-breaking moment for us, especially as she was also desperately worried about Dougie, her other son, who was still with the 14th Army in Burma.

In the several weeks to Christmas, we were invited to a small reception one evening at the New Wheel Hotel in the village. John was presented with a bankbook containing money given from the Wrenthorpe Village Forces Fund. This was a really generous gesture, considering he had not lived there for four and a half years. A week or two later a similar reception was given for him by Stanley Council at the Wheel Hotel, Bradford Road and given another bank book with money from the Council Fund for Servicemen.

In the late summer of 1942, after the disastrous North-African news, the Yorkshire Evening News (now Post) realised that many of its readers would have sons and husbands who were now Prisoners of War and started a POW Club. There were branches in most Yorkshire towns which met once a month in a pub or hotel. These were for relatives to discuss ways to raise funds and to send parcels to their men-folk. The Wakefield branch met at what was then the Great Bull Hotel at the top of Westgate.

Only three from Wakefield arrived home that November - Norman Bramham, Alec Easter and John - all the others were still being held in German camps. The three were invited to attend the meeting to receive inscribed cigarette lighters as a welcome home gift. However, when they were asked to get up on the concert room stage to say a few words, Norman and Alec headed smartly for the exit, leaving John to get up, totally embarrassed, in front of about 200 ladies, to thank them for all their fund-raising efforts.

He did receive a parcel of I think 500 cigarettes, at Camp 70. He was able to trade these for bread as he never smoked, when almost everyone did then. We still have the lighter which is still unused after all these years.

Despite my having to work our happiness was complete in those weeks before Christmas. This was marred only by the prospect of his instructions to report to Otley on the 16th, and the prospect of us being parted for yet another Christmas. To our great joy a letter came on the 14th from the York Records Office giving John an extension until 2nd January, a lovely gesture from the Army which was much appreciated.

A letter also arrived from Margaret in Horton telling us that Jim was getting Christmas leave and asking if we would like to spend it with them. So - off we went for a memorable holiday - as I had also been allowed time off until the New Year. A most happy reunion for John happened when Jim stepped off the train on Horton station. This began for us an unforgettable old fashioned Dales Christmas, during which we all may have over-indulged with the food and drink - but who would have blamed us?

Then we came back home to reality, with the start of the new year being very cold and frosty. John starting to be rehabilitated, as the Army called it, running up and down the by then, snowy hillsides round Otley. In fact, so much of it that his left knee, which had been troubling him ever since his Cyprus days, finally gave up on him. He was whisked off to Pinderfields Hospital for a cartilage operation. Amazing - what incredible luck for us! It turned out to be a stay of several weeks and, with the hospital being only a mile from home, we were again re-united. We managed to see a lot of each other on my evening visits and then at home when he was able to walk.

In mid-March he was given a week of leave and, explaining the situation at work, I was allowed another week off, without pay of course. So we took off for Blackpool, calling it a very late honeymoon and had a marvellous holiday, in spite of the cold weather.

Around mid-April John was discharged from hospital and sent to a rehab camp for ex-POWs in Halifax. He considered this more like a punishment camp with the emphasis on physical fitness – especially for those returning from liberated German camps, among them some from his own unit. In the end he was actually punished for being absent on an unauthorised weekend at home. He returned to find himself in trouble and was given seven days 'confined to camp'. The next day was the 8th May - Victory in Europe (VE) Day. He spent it doing cook-house chores, but the following day the 'sentence' was quashed - leaving him without a stain on his army career.

Shortly after this he took another medical and was passed as fully fit. The war in the Far East was still going on and he was sent with several others to a barracks in Scotland on a course of general training. This was run by staff from the 9th Battalion Bedfordshire and Hertfordshire Regiment. This gave me the anxious feeling that he could be sent overseas again but, thankfully, this didn't happen.

Other married men at the Barracks were having their wives to stay in the locality and were granted sleeping-out passes. So, with the war obviously coming nearer to its end, I was granted another two weeks of compassionate leave to go to Scotland. This was to be towards the end of July and, never having travelled so far before or on my own, the train journey to Glasgow was horrible. It was packed with servicemen and I had to stand all the way - not one man having offered me a seat.

Happily, John was able to meet me in Glasgow before the further 20-mile journey to the village of Balloch, which was at the southern end of Loch Lomond. He had managed to book lodgings for me in a nice family bungalow just a mile from the Barracks. I was fortunate in having another army wife for company until John arrived after duty. She was Evelyn Jefferson from Bridlington, wife of Cyril (Jeff) who had returned from a German POW camp - John having met him again in Halifax.

There is not much more I can add to John's story. The war was officially over with the Japanese surrender, which came during my holiday. John returned to his unit at Kirby Moorside with the possibility of a posting to join the Occupation Forces in the Far East, as he was not due for demob for another nine months. The Army finally used common sense and allowed him early release for his work in the building trade.

After six years of uncertainty and the struggle just to survive along with millions of others we could at last look forward with confidence to our future. Our only regret is never having been blessed with children. In our younger days there wasn't the fertility treatment available today, but we're very content with all our memories, and very happy to have survived so long and are very content in our sheltered bungalow.

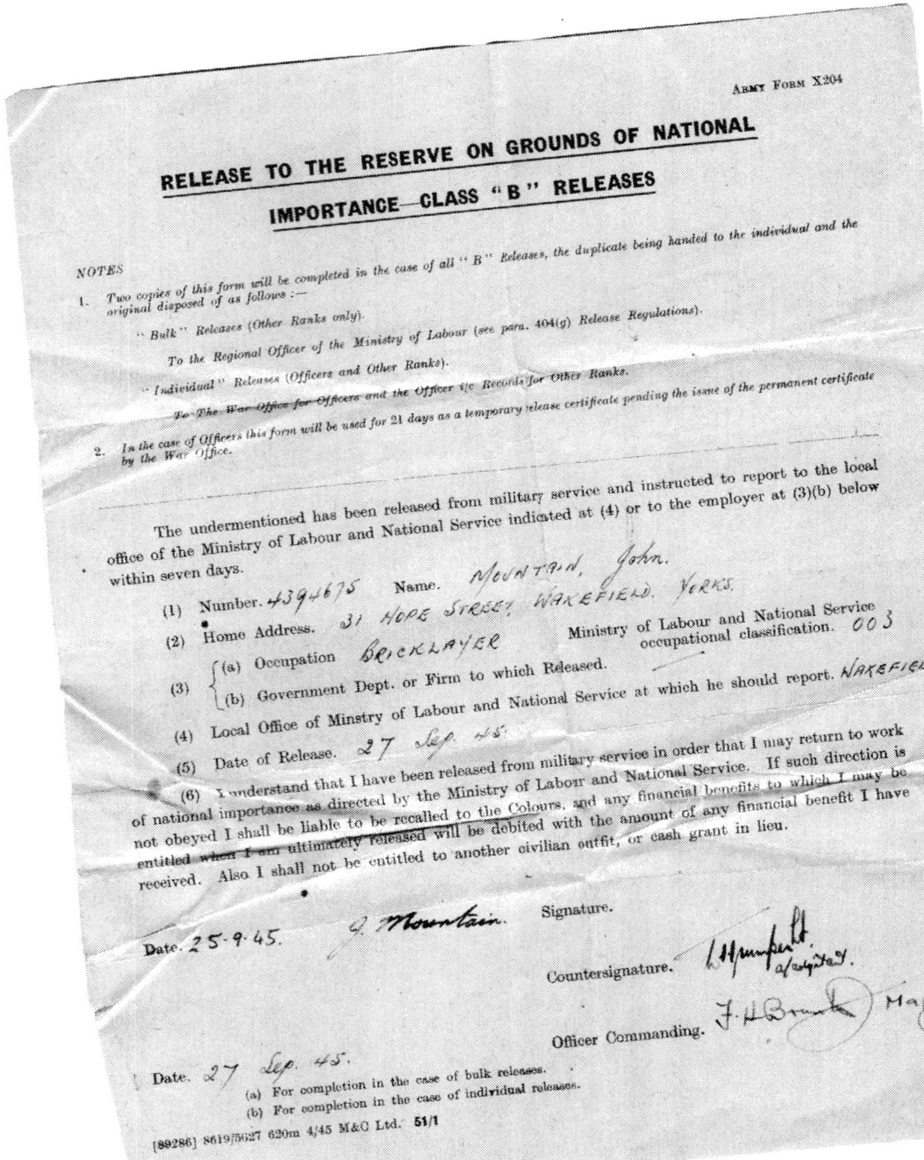

ARMY FORM X204

RELEASE TO THE RESERVE ON GROUNDS OF NATIONAL IMPORTANCE—CLASS "B" RELEASES

NOTES

1. Two copies of this form will be completed in the case of all "B" Releases, the duplicate being handed to the individual and the original disposed of as follows :—

"Bulk" Releases (Other Ranks only).

To the Regional Officer of the Ministry of Labour (see para. 404(g) Release Regulations).

"Individual" Releases (Officers and Other Ranks).

To The War Office for Officers and the Officer i/c Records for Other Ranks.

2. In the case of Officers this form will be used for 21 days as a temporary release certificate pending the issue of the permanent certificate by the War Office.

The undermentioned has been released from military service and instructed to report to the local office of the Ministry of Labour and National Service indicated at (4) or to the employer at (3)(b) below within seven days.

(1) Number. *439-4675*   Name. *MOUNTAIN, John.*

(2) Home Address. *31 HOPE STREET, WAKEFIELD. YORKS.*

(3) (a) Occupation *BRICKLAYER*   Ministry of Labour and National Service occupational classification. *003*

(b) Government Dept. or Firm to which Released. _____

(4) Local Office of Ministry of Labour and National Service at which he should report. *WAKEFIELD.*

(5) Date of Release. *27 Sep. 45.*

(6) I understand that I have been released from military service in order that I may return to work of national importance as directed by the Ministry of Labour and National Service. If such direction is not obeyed I shall be liable to be recalled to the Colours, and any financial benefits to which I may be entitled when I am ultimately released will be debited with the amount of any financial benefit I have received. Also I shall not be entitled to another civilian outfit, or cash grant in lieu.

Date. *25-9-45.*   *J. Mountain.*   Signature.

Countersignature. *L Humphell a/cap Sdy.*

Officer Commanding. *J. H. Brunt) Major.*

Date. *27 Sep. 45.*

(a) For completion in the case of bulk releases.

(b) For completion in the case of individual releases.

[89286] 8619/5627 620m 4/45 M&C Ltd. 51/1

Fig 31: John's army release note

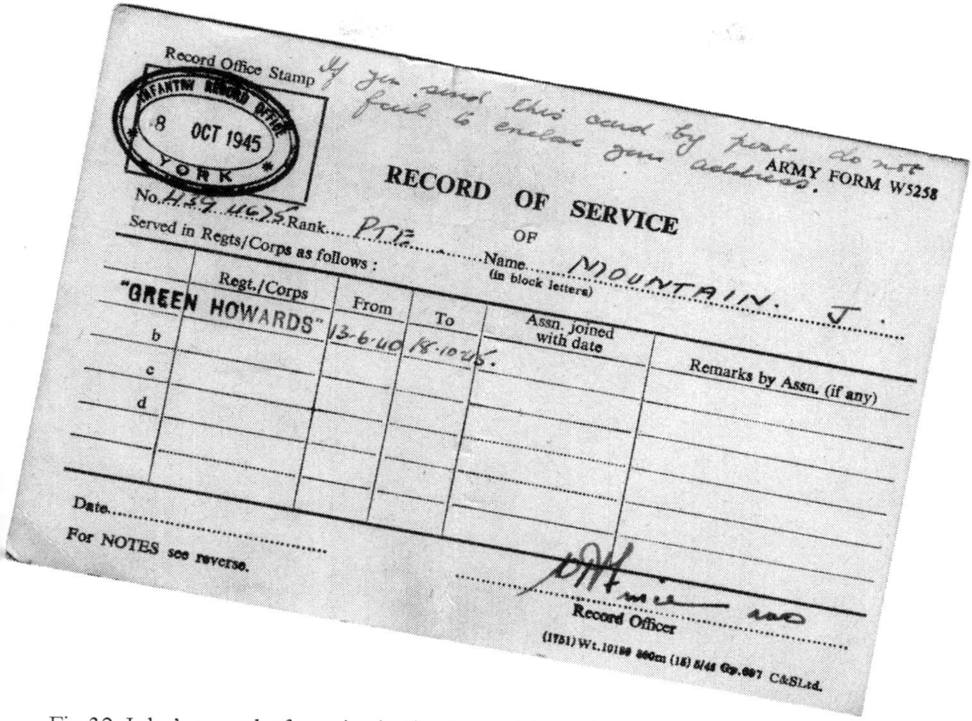

Record Office Stamp

INFANTRY RECORD OFFICE
8 OCT 1945
YORK

If you send this card by post do not fail to enclose your address.

ARMY FORM W5258

RECORD OF SERVICE

OF

No. 4394675 Rank PTE

Name MOUNTAIN. J.
(in block letters)

Served in Regts/Corps as follows :

	Regt./Corps	From	To	Assn. joined with date	Remarks by Assn. (if any)
	"GREEN HOWARDS"	13-6-40	18-10-45.		
b					
c					
d					

Date.................................

For NOTES see reverse.

Record Officer

(1751) Wt.10189 800m (16) 8/45 Gp.687 C&S Ltd.

Fig 32: John's record of service in the Green Howards

Len Hartley, John's school friend
who was shot down over Belgium
in September 1944

Dedication

This book is in memory of our dear friend, John Leonard Hartley and the many thousands who sacrificed their lives.

John would like to quote a poem, written in the trenches of the First World War, that he learned in the Libyan desert.

Dear to me ever, thy countryside,

But dearer now for the men who died,

Robbed of the richest of Youths' long years,

Steeling their hearts to a mother's tears,

Fighting their way through a thousand Hells,

Wearing a cross like a cap and bells,

Jeering at death as a last grim joke,

My thanks go up with the thin blue smoke,

Marking the cottage that's home to me,

In the dear safe land by the shining sea.

Whilst producing this book it has come to light that this verse is based on a section of 'Demobilised' by G.A. Studdert Kennedy.

His collected verse is published in an out-of-print work; The Unutterable Beauty - published by Hodder & Stoughton

Appendix A - Maps

The following maps were added with the second edition to try and help the reader to understand the distances John travels in the book.

Map 1 (p.163) shows the route across the Atlantic Ocean on board HM Troop Ship Mooltan and up the east coast of Africa on the Mauritania.

Map 2 (p.164) shows the locations John passed through prior to his capture in Egypt.

Map 3 (p.165) shows the route through Italy - both as a POW, as an escapee and then the route towards home after the liberation of France.

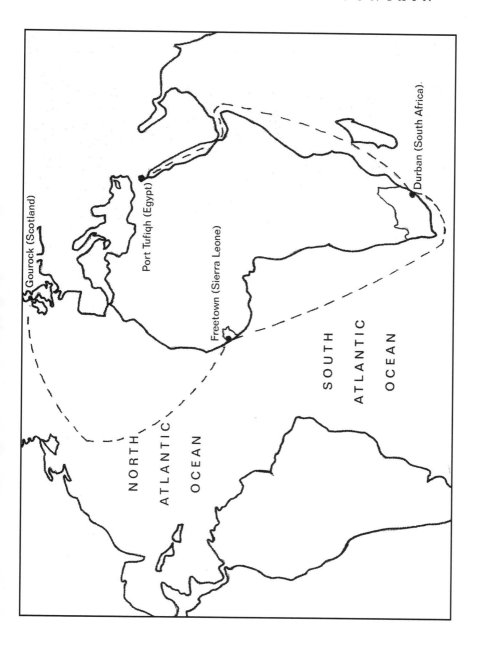

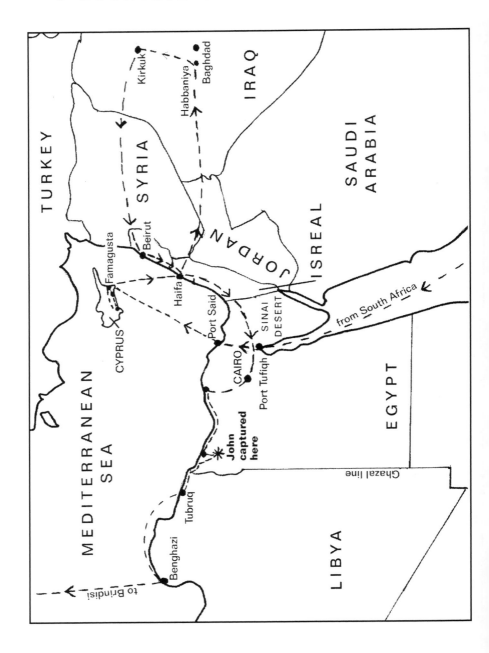

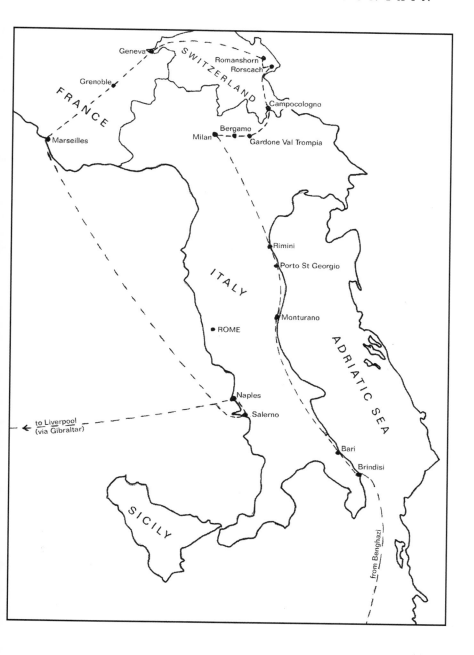

3422761R00091

Printed in Great Britain
by Amazon.co.uk, Ltd.,
Marston Gate.